Blairsville Junior High School
Blairsville, Pennsylvania

THE BYZANTINES

THE BYZANTINES

BY THOMAS CALDECOT CHUBB

ILLUSTRATED BY *Richard M. Powers*

THE WORLD PUBLISHING COMPANY

CLEVELAND AND NEW YORK

Published by The World Publishing Company
2231 West 110th Street, Cleveland 2, Ohio

Published simultaneously in Canada by
Nelson, Foster & Scott Ltd.

Library of Congress Catalog Card Number: 59–5919

For Rosamond Caldecot Chubb

CONTENTS

*Pronunciations for unfamiliar words
are given in the Index*

THE BYZANTINES

A CRUSADE THAT WENT ASTRAY

More than 750 years ago—the exact date was May 24, 1203—
a mighty and crowded armada sailed away from the beautiful
island of Corfu just off the northwest corner of Greece.

It headed southward toward a brilliant blue sea.

The weather was balmy. The myrtle was in bloom. The
leaves on the twisted gray olive trees flashed silver. The sky
was fine and clear. The wind was gentle and favorable. Indeed, it barely ruffled the water. But it filled hundreds and

hundreds of sails of every possible color. Red sails. Golden sails. Lavender sails. Green sails. Orange sails. And sails of a wonderful bright yellow. Even Geoffrey of Villehardouin, a bold French baron and famous historian who was one of the passengers, could not say how many they were. But he did know that they took his breath away.

"I, Geoffrey," he scratched out slowly, "to my knowledge have not ever lied by one word, and I bear witness that never was yet seen so fair a sight. As far as the eye could reach, there was no space without sails, and ships, and vessels."

Certainly there were enough ships to cover miles of ocean. Flat, broad-beamed palanders, built especially to carry troops and horses—the 4,500 knights with their fiery steeds, the 9,000 esquires, and the 20,000 foot soldiers who made up the expedition.

Swift galleys to protect the mighty convoy. These galleys had oars as well as sails, and they lashed the waters to foam as they hurried about their tasks. There were even some fat, slow merchant vessels. Just as it is today, business was business in the Middle Ages, even when you went to war.

But business or no business, the men crowding the rails were carried forward by another, nobler purpose. And before each of them had left his drafty castle in Normandy or France or Italy, he had sworn this solemn oath: "I will put on the cross, and march to redeem the land where Jesus lived, and where He died for us."

Once before it had been redeemed by Godfrey of Bouillon and the other saints and heroes of the First Crusade. But then the famous Arab leader Saladin had won it back, and not even Richard the Lion-Hearted, the knightly king of England, could defeat Saladin.

"We will succeed where Richard failed. *Deus vult!* God wills it!"

The crusaders had a plan. Instead of landing on the enemy-held beaches of Palestine, they would sail to Egypt and fight their way across the desert and up through the famous Gaza strip, about which we read even today, to Jerusalem. The back door would be easier than the front door. They could not fail.

Their hearts, therefore, were high as they sailed along the rugged coast with its deep inlets and its violet mountains— past rocky Ithaca, the legendary home of the wily Ulysses; past yellow beaches where the ancient Greeks drew up their craft before they sailed to rescue Helen of Troy; finally, past the southernmost tip of Greece where the storms were supposed to meet. Then suddenly something happened. Instead of continuing toward the Holy Land, the mighty fleet altered its course and turned north. What possibly could be the reason? The leaders knew, but most of the fighting men were puzzled.

Soon a whisper ran from lip to lip. There was a new destination. Constantinople the Golden—the fabled Byzantium! The capital of the Greek, or Eastern Roman, Empire! The legendary El Dorado city with its glitter and its glory which was set on the Bosporus, a narrow little body of water that divides Europe from Asia, separating the West from the East.

It was the tough old doge of Venice who had changed the crusaders' minds for them. Henry Dandolo was eighty years old and blind, but he knew that ducats did not grow on trees, and he was just as eager to get back the money he had loaned them as any Venetian merchant over whom he ruled. The crusaders had promised to give the Venetians four silver marks for each man and two silver marks for each horse that they transported to the East, but now after months of borrowing and begging and promising instead of paying, they still owed them 34,000 marks. What could be done about it?

Facing the knights and barons in the great, glittering church of Saint Mark, the old doge stroked his white beard and had an answer. "You are fighting men. Pay us back with fighting. The king of Hungary has taken Zara from us. Take it back again and give it to us."

They did, but even then the Venetians were not satisfied.

"There is a richer prize ahead. Win us Constantinople. Capture *it* for us, and we will really call quits."

The leaders agreed. The Holy Land would have to wait a while to be redeemed.

It would be impossible to exaggerate the excitement of the crusaders when they heard the magic name of Constantinople. For they all knew about the fabulous city. Minstrels told about it in the long sagas they sang before huge crackling fires on winter nights. They spoke of its shining metal towers and called it Micklegarth, or Bigtown.

Its fame was also spread throughout the West by Russian traders. In those days, the Russians were like the vikings who roved the oceans from America to the Greek Sea. They had enslaved the backward Slavic tribes of Kiev and Moscow and once a year, when the ice melted, these snub-nosed, green-eyed marauders made their vassals cut down huge trees and hollow them into boats. Aboard these, they floated down the great rivers, and then sailed across the foggy Black Sea and up the Bosporus until they reached the enormous city, the biggest they had ever seen. There they traded honey and marten skins and dried fish and even caviar for pepper and brocades and carved ivory and delicate enamels. These Russians, too, were dazzled by Constantinople and had their own name for it. They called it Tsargrad, or Caesar City.

But long before there were Russians or any other kind of vikings, the city had amazed our ancestors. "I see before my eyes something I had often heard about but would never believe!" exclaimed Athanaric, a guttural-speaking king from the forests of Germany. "Look at the walls. Look at the buildings, look at the harbor filled with ships! Look at the men of every nation crowding the alleys and bazaars. Look at the disciplined soldiers! Surely God himself must be the emperor!" said Athanaric.

The mighty Charlemagne, who had been crowned emperor of the West, once sent an embassy to Constantinople to discuss the possibility of marrying the Byzantine empress Irene. Rabbi Benjamin of Tudela, a learned Spanish Jew, was astonished at its splendor. It was richer, he said, than any other city in the world. Why, the ordinary merchant wore garments of silk ornamented with gold and precious stones! He rode about his business on horseback as a prince does!

It was the city of Justinian, the great lawgiver, whose book of laws was still studied in the crusaders' own cities of Paris and Bologna 700 years after his reign.

Only the wisest of them knew that he was much more than a lawgiver. A tall towheaded country boy from what is modern Yugoslavia, he was more than just one of the great Byzantine emperors. He was one of the great rulers of all time. It was his generals who reconquered Africa, Italy, and parts of Spain, and almost restored the ancient Roman Empire. It was he who ordered the most famous architects of the time to build the church of Santa Sophia. Most of the finest Byzantine mosaics were done during his reign, and the Orthodox Christian Church was first firmly established then. The Age of Justinian was the first great age of the Byzantine Empire when its power affected the whole Mediterranean world.

It was the city of great soldiers like the cruel Basil the Bulgar Slayer, who had cold-bloodedly blinded 15,000 of his Bulgarian enemies, but who had permanently broken the power of these wild raiders; like John Kercuas, an Asia Minor

Napoleon; and like Nicephorus Phocas, who had rolled back the Arabs, the deadliest foes of the Byzantines, whether they fought on camel back or on a warship at sea.

It was the city of foxy Alexius Comnenus, and his dark-eyed daughter, Anna, who wrote even better histories than Villehardouin.

The crusaders knew about *him!* By his quick thinking and crafty talking this same Alexius, Emperor Alexius I, had not

only persuaded their grandsires and great-grandsires of an earlier crusade to stay out of Constantinople, but he had also talked them into fighting the Turks for him. He had even talked some of them into becoming his vassals. He had received the leaders in the Sacred Palace, however, and they told the other barons what they saw there. From then on Constantinople was a city of marvels to the men of the Middle Ages. They also began to covet its wealth.

To be sure, not all the crusaders were happy at the thought of attacking another Christian city, especially when they remembered how angry the Pope had been at the taking of Zara, also a Christian city. But the doge of Venice had an answer for every objection.

The Byzantines, the people of Constantinople, were not really true Christians at all, he said. They were heretics.

The crusaders were not conquering Constantinople; they were restoring it to its rightful ruler. On board was the young Alexius, who ought to sit on the throne as Alexius IV. Alexius was a worthless young man, but his father had been emperor until he was deposed and blinded by his own brother.

Besides that, how could the crusaders pay back Venice all they owed her if they did not take Constantinople?

The young Alexius not only promised that he would settle all their debts if they took the city for him, but that he would give them enough money to go on to their destination. He said that he would ride with them at the head of a Byzantine army of 10,000 soldiers. He promised that as long as he lived he would equip and maintain out of his own treasury 500 of their knights.

A majority of the brave knights were convinced by these arguments and by the thought of all the fighting men and gold. Among them was Geoffrey of Villehardouin who tells us most of what we know about the Fourth Crusade.

It took almost a month tó make the voyage. After the crusaders rounded the tip of Greece, they sailed past the remains of ancient Sparta, past Athens, and at the island of Andros they stopped for water. A little later, they drifted past the site of the ancient town of Troy. Finally, they touched at Abydos on the historic Dardanelles, where they raided the countryside and filled their holds with grain. "Great was the need thereof!" muttered Geoffrey.

On June 23, 1203, they dropped anchor within sight of Constantinople. The snow-covered Thracian mountains lay to the west, and grape-colored Asia Minor to starboard. "And be it known to you," scratched out Villehardouin, his pulses beating, "that no man among us was so hardy that he did not tremble." For in every direction, there was nothing but high walls and towers and rich palaces and mighty churches.

The next morning banners and pennants were flown from the castles of every ship. The coverings were taken from the shields. The bulwarks were made ready for action. Then the sailors weighed anchor and spread sails to the wind.

"Thus we passed before Constantinople and so near that we shot at their vessels. There were so many people on the walls and towers that it seemed as if there could be no more people in the world."

Four weeks later the city was in their hands, and although Geoffrey and his fellow crusaders did not realize it, this event marked a turning point in history. For 900 years Constantinople had stood proudly and safe, ruling her empire and giving orders like a queen. But from now on she would be at the mercy of others.

That is not what Geoffrey and his companions were thinking about as they rode into the fabled streets, however. They were remembering all they had heard about the magic city. They were wondering if even half of it was true.

BYZANTIUM,
CROSSROADS OF THE WORLD

They found that it was true indeed.

On that hot July day when the crusaders and Venetians at last forced their way with young Alexius into Constantinople, it was neither as rich nor as powerful as it had been when the earlier Alexius let the leaders of the First Crusade cool their heels outside its gates more than a hundred years before.

But if you wanted to find a more fabulous city, you would have had to go all the way across Asia to distant Cathay. There, of course, was Khansa (modern Hangchow), which was so enormous that it took one medieval traveler three days merely to cross from one side of it to the other. There, too, was Khan Baliq (modern Peking) where "twice five miles of fertile ground with walls and towers were girdled round" just to make a playground for the Chinese Son of Heaven, or emperor. But since Marco Polo would not even be born for another fifty years, most of the crusaders knew very little about Cathay, that is, if they had even heard of it at all!

Their idea of a big city was London with its gloomy smoke-blackened houses, and in those days London was really a little town. Even Westminster Abbey was a mile in the country and surrounded by green fields. Or Paris with its streets so narrow that you could hardly see the sky between overhanging gables, and with the great Cathedral of Notre Dame not yet finished. Paris hardly extended a mile in any direction. Or Bruges with its bent and wizened wool merchants and the damp smell of its canals. Even Rome, the most famous city in the West, could not have had much more than 30,000 inhabitants. Most of these were ruffians and bandits who robbed pilgrims, fought each other, and even battled the Pope from castles made of marble stolen from the ancient monuments.

But Constantinople, at the crossroads of the world, gleamed in the sun and was proud and mighty. Even then it had a population of at least 800,000. Possibly a million people lived there.

They were of every kind and race, for like modern New York, the Byzantine city was a melting pot.

Swarthy Armenians looking for the fortune that had enabled more than one of their number to mount the Byzantine throne.

Intellectual Greek scholars moving toward the lecture room with a precious copy of Plato or Aristotle under their arms.

Blond-haired Anglo-Saxons, described by one who saw them to be "tall as palm trees." Ever since William the Conqueror had ruled in England, they had come in growing numbers to join the famous Varangians, or imperial bodyguard.

Russian traders bursting out of their own Saint Mamas quarter in the city to drink the unfamiliar Greek wine which made them quarrel and brawl.

Strikingly handsome Asbagians from Colchis, the land of the legendary Golden Fleece, and probably of rich placer gold mines almost like the ones in California.

Jewish merchants from the Pera quarter, on the other side of the Golden Horn. They were not allowed to live in the city itself which they had to reach by water, and they were often oppressed and persecuted; but they were rich, benevolent, and pious.

Unwashed, but shaven Bulgarians, who wore an iron chain for a belt.

Wild, half-Mongol Patzinaks, and somewhat more civilized Khazars from the Ukraine and the Caucasus.

Dark-eyed Asiatics with pointed beards and black hair, and usually wearing turbans, who had come by camel caravan from Syria or even Baghdad.

Iranians. Spaniards. Copts from ancient Egypt. Ethiopians from fabled Axum. Franks and Lombards. In the old days, there might also have been Indians and men from China, but no longer. Bankers and sea captains from Amalfi, Pisa, and Genoa. The latter in particular looked about them nervously. They could not help wondering what their fate would be now that their archenemy and rival, Venice, had taken over.

Finally, there were the Byzantines themselves. Proud and haughty noblemen with strange titles you could hardly pronounce. These noblemen moved through the streets arrogantly and did not seem to know that their great days were over. Sometimes a slave walked beside them, carrying a bright-colored umbrella or parasol. Lovely ladies, beautifully dressed, jeweled and painted, and probably with a smile for the tall, fair-haired northerners. Byzantine families, the wife on a donkey, the husband and children on foot. Fierce-eyed monks, of whom there were more than 30,000, and priests who swarmed everywhere, led by their hegumens and archimandrites. And, of course, the famous Byzantine peddlers with their purposely ragged clothes, gesticulating hands, and whining cries. The place was still a happy hunting ground for hucksters.

"The city guarded by God"—the name given by the Byzantines to Constantinople—was big enough to hold all of them and splendid enough to make them glad that it could.

A medieval traveler said that the circumference of its walls was eighteen miles, and although he was probably just as good at telling tall stories as present-day travelers are, he may have been right. At least if you included such flourishing suburbs as Galata (once called Sycae, or Figtrees) and Scutari (formerly Chrysopolis, or Gold City). Galata (like Pera) and Scutari were separated from Constantinople by the Golden Horn and the Bosporus, respectively, which were narrow bodies of water, not as wide as the Hudson River or the East River at New York City.

Constantinople itself was large enough. Like old Rome, New Rome (for that was its official name; Constantinople, or Constantine's City, was only a nickname which had stuck) sprawled over seven rolling hills and down to every body of water it could find.

That was what a visitor remembered most about Constantinople: One was never far from the water. It was shaped like a hitchhiker's thumb pointed toward the shore of Asia Minor, and it was bounded by sea on every side except where the thumb joined the hand. On the north was the famous Golden Horn—an arm of the Bosporus—which is still a wonderful har-

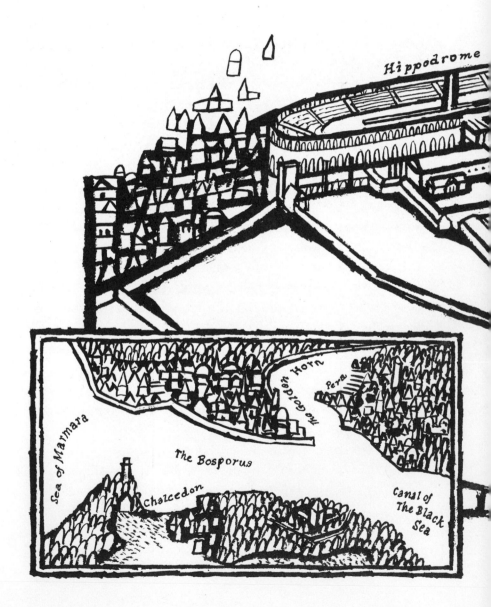

Hippodrome

Sea of Marmara

The Bosporus

Chalcedon

The Golden Horn

Pera

Canal of The Black Sea

IN CONSTANTINOPLE

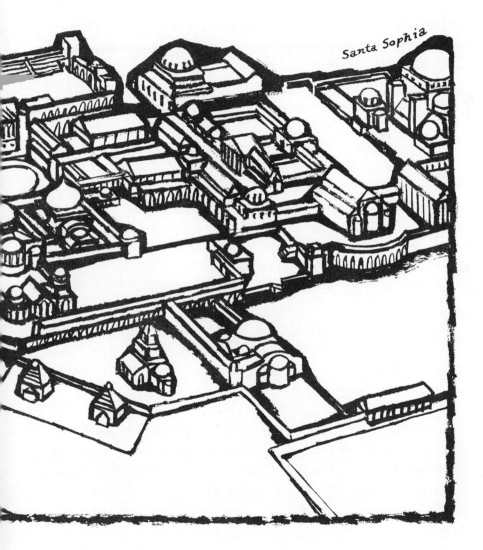

Santa Sophia

bor. It is so deep that ships can moor with their prows against the warehouses ashore and still be comfortably afloat. On the north and northeast was the narrow Bosporus with its twisting channel and its dangerous currents. Jason and his Argonauts had supposedly sailed through the Bosporus. On the southeast and south was the Sea of Marmara. On the Marmara shore there were many small man-made harbors, at least one of which was reserved for the emperor. Through the Sea of Marmara, one could reach to the Dardanelles, the Aegean Sea, and finally the Mediterranean; and then on to Egypt, the Red Sea, and India in one direction, and to Spain and even England in the other.

Guarded by these seas and by the great walls which protected it from the west, some of which still stand, was an *Arabian Nights'* fantasy of lovely vales and gardens, glittering roofs and towers, and, of course, resplendent buildings that were beyond anything that the adventurers from the cold and foggy north could even imagine.

Among the crusaders was another knight who could write as well as fight. His name was Robert of Clari.

"I do not think," said Robert, "that in the forty richest cities of the world there is as much treasure. In fact, the Greeks said that two-thirds of all the wealth there is, is in Constantinople. The rest is scattered elsewhere."

Then he went into details.

Most glittering of all, he noted, was the Palace of Bukoleon. "Within it," he said, "there were fully five hundred halls, all connected with one another and all made with gold mosaic. In it, there were fully thirty chapels. One of them was called the Holy Chapel, which was so rich and noble that there was not a hinge or band or any part such as is usually made of iron that was not all of silver. And there was no column that was not of jasper or of porphyry or some other precious stone."

The Palace of Bukoleon had got its name from a statue showing a fight between a bull and a lion. It had been the Great, or Sacred, Palace of the earlier emperors. It covered 25 or 30 acres and was really a collection of buildings, for a Byzantine palace was never a single edifice.

There were too many buildings in the Great Palace to tell you about all of them. Among them was the Daphne Palace. It was the oldest one, having been built by Constantine the Great when he founded the city. There was the Building of the Nineteen Beds where the emperor could hold a state dinner for 218 important people. Another building was the Chalké where the emperor received his parade troops. It was 650 feet long, and in the old days it was guarded by Khazars with drawn bows. It got its name because its roof was a huge sheet of polished copper. A fourth building was the Magnaura, or Fresh Breeze, Palace where the empress went in stately procession to take her ceremonial baths.

It was at the Magnaura Palace that an Italian visitor discovered what the Byzantines would do to impress strangers. Liutprand, the bishop of Cremona, was led before the emperor, whom he found seated upon a golden throne. There he was told to bow himself three times, each time with his face to the ground.

He did so; then he looked up. No emperor.

By a clever device, the latter had been lifted to the ceiling, and now clad in entirely new clothes, he looked down upon the bishop. In the meantime, gilded mechanical birds began to sing, and gilded bronze lions beat the ground with their tails and roared terribly with open mouth and quivering tongues.

Part of the palace group, too, was the renowned church of

Santa Sophia. It was known as the Great Church, and although it was not as big as Saint Peter's in Rome, it was one of
the largest sacred buildings ever made by man. Even today,
with most of its mosaics covered with whitewash—this was
done by the Turks—it is like nothing else in the world. To
Robert of Clari, its great height, equivalent to a modern
eighteen-story building, its many chapels, its lacelike balcon-
ies, and its beautifully carved pillars made it like the work
of an enchanter. Its dome was so vast that the architects had
to try twice before they could make one that would not fall
down. When they did, it was so graceful that it seemed to be
floating on air.

But what impressed Robert of Clari most of all was its
more-than-Oriental splendor. The principal altar was beyond
price, he said. The altar table was 14 feet long. It was made
of gold and precious stones crushed up together. Above it was
a solid silver canopy held up by solid silver columns. The
whole ceiling was overlaid with pure gold. Robert did not

even speak of the mosaics which we now know were as fine as any ever made, but he did say that there were more than 200 chandeliers. Each of these had twenty-five or more lamps, and was hung from a silver chain as thick as a man's arm.

Last but not least of the palace buildings was the Hippodrome, or Circus. This was a tremendous stadium about 2,000 feet long and 600 feet wide. On three sides of it were thirty or forty rows of seats, and at the north end was the Cathisma, or balcony, where the emperor and empress sat in state. It must have held 100,000 people.

In the days of old the Hippodrome was the center of almost every kind of citizen activity. Here were held wildly exciting chariot races during which the Green and Blue factions (they were like the Democrats and Republicans in the United States) forgot their politics to bet on their favorites, and were ready to fly at each other with stones or swords if the wrong one got ahead. Here there were wild beast fights, bearbaiting, acrobatic feats, performances by clowns, jugglers, trained dogs, and even a trained, gilded crocodile. But not fights by gladiators, for the Christian Byzantines did not think it was right for one man to kill another in the name of sport.

Here, too, the emperor-elect stood to hear the crowds proclaim him, and it was here that more than once he had to face the people and promise to obey his own laws. Some very bloody riots, called the Nika revolt, started at the Hippodrome, and it was there that they were put down with a loss of 30,000 lives.

But Robert of Clari did not limit his sightseeing to the Great Palace and its grounds. He went everywhere. He visited the new Palace of Blachernae by the Golden Horn and saw that it was almost as splendid as the Bukoleon, even though it had *only* twenty chapels and two or three hundred chambers! He stood at the Golden Gate with its two life-sized elephants made of copper. This gate was only opened when the emperor, called the Augustus, returned from a victory. Then he was taken through it seated on a golden throne on a golden four-wheeled chariot. The clergy scattered incense, and the crowd shouted, "Life eternal to our holy Augustus!"

Robert also saw the Gate of the Golden Mantle with its shining globe which was supposed to protect the city from being destroyed by lightning. A statue on the globe proclaimed in large letters: "Anyone who lives in Constantinople a year can be rich enough to afford a golden mantle like the one I wear."

He saw the great monument to Justinian. It towered into the air, and on top of it was a bronze statue of this mighty emperor. He was on horseback and wore a headdress very much like that of an Aztec chieftain.

He also saw the holy relics with which the city was filled—two pieces of the true cross, the head of the lance that pierced Christ's side, two of the nails used in the Crucifixion, a vial containing the Saviour's blood, the tunic that He wore on the first Good Friday, the crown of thorns itself, and the famous "handkerchief of Edessa" on which His portrait had been imprinted by a miracle.

Last of all, Robert of Clari gawked at the two columns each of which prophesied the city's doom. "Even our coming was predicted," he said.

But no one in Constantinople understood what the ships and soldiers on the columns meant until the crusaders were actually there. Then the frightened people realized that short-haired warriors with iron swords would come from the West to conquer them. By that time, it was too late.

But there was much more to this Byzantine city than palaces and monuments and churches. It was a city of people as well as the city of the emperor, and it was all noise and excitement, hustle and bustle, and activity.

No part of it was busier than the long avenue that started at the Augustaion, or Emperor Square, in front of Santa Sophia, and went three or four miles to the city walls. It was called the Mesé, or Midway, and it was really like a modern midway in the variety of wares it offered.

Here, for example, under its colonnades and porticoes were the workbenches of the goldsmiths. In plain sight of everybody, they manufactured lovely gold boxes, gold jewelry, and intricate enamel. Near the goldsmiths were the money changers with their long tables or banks heaped with the coin of every nation. Next came the provision sellers, those who sold every kind of food from meat and cheese to bread and honey. The sellers of silk had their booths between the Forum of Constantine and the Taurus Forum, with its tall column and statue of Theodosius. The perfume sellers did their business in front of the Great Palace. In other places—but I could not name them all—there was a bazaar so filled with gleaming wares that it was called the house of lamps, a street of the tinsmiths and coppersmiths, a bazaar for household goods, a pig-and-sheep market, a cattle market, and, of course, a horse market.

Noisier than all the others, and more filled with bargaining in twenty Near East languages was the fish market, located on the quays by the Golden Horn.

The Mesé was a respectable place and one was safe, at least in daylight, when visiting the booths and markets; but to go anywhere else in the city was another matter. To be sure, there was nothing in the world as magnificent as the glitter and the gold of Caesar City. But outside of the native quarter in a city in Algiers or Morocco, there were no slums like the slums of Constantinople. They spread all over, covering acre after acre of ground, and they made up a miserable network of filthy side streets and dark, damp, and dirty tenements. There was absolutely no sanitation. The gutters were the only sewers. Household refuse, including spoiled meat and vegetables and ancient and decaying fish, were thrown out of slitlike windows to be trampled under foot by every passerby. In rainy weather the mud was more than ankle deep. One can imagine how it smelled.

Here lived the working population of the city—porters with calluses on their hands and padded coats, donkey drivers with shrill cries and quick, short steps like those that can be seen even today in many a city in the Balkans. Carpenters. Water carriers. Day laborers. Here too lived an even more wretched riffraff who lived off doles and charity, when they didn't live off murder and crime. Here was the poor creature with sore eyes who sat with his wooden begging bowl in front of a church or on the sunny side of a square. Here was a one-eyed scoundrel who would cut throats for a copper obol. Yet sometimes they gathered together and formed a mob that marched to the Hippodrome and demanded a new emperor, and more than once they got what they wanted.

This was what Constantinople was like in the late Middle Ages and for 600 years before that. But it was also much more than a seething pot of emperors and rich men, poor men, beggarmen, and thieves.

It was the capital of a very famous empire which took over the eastern half of the old Roman Empire and became known as the Byzantine Empire because it stood on the site of the ancient Greek city of Byzantium. In spite of all its enemies, this empire lasted 1,123 years and eighteen days. And at a

THE EMPIRE

UNDER

JUSTINIAN

550 A.D.

A F

time when half a dozen other empires crumbled, including ancient Persia and ancient Rome!

Sometimes it was a very big empire indeed. Under the mighty Justinian it ruled from the Euphrates, which flows into the distant Persian Gulf, to the Straits of Gibraltar, and from the Nile in one direction and the Crimea of South Russia in the other to Switzerland. It ruled all of Italy, and all of the Balkans, and all of Asia Minor, and all North Africa.

Sometimes the empire was so small that it was little more than the city itself.

But whether it was big or little, it was almost always the most important and the strongest nation west of China. Sometimes it was the only important one!

How did it get that way?

How was it able to keep strong when so much of the rest of the world was breaking into pieces?

What did it do for the world? For it did a great deal.

Why should you and I care about Constantinople and the Byzantine Empire?

I will try to tell you.

The ROMAN EMPIRE AND CONSTANTINOPLE

The beginning of the story took place a long time ago, and not even in the same land.

Back in the days when our ancestors still dressed in skins and hides and had just given up stone weapons for bronze, a group of people moved out of central Europe to the north of Italy. They stayed there for a thousand years, made pottery and grew beans, beets, barley, and millet and finally learned how to use iron. They also grazed cattle and herded sheep, and so one day when they learned that the coastland from the Tiber River to the Bay of Naples was so lush with tall green grass that it was called Vitelia (the name Italy comes from mispronouncing this), or Calfland, they moved south again.

There they settled in the rugged blue hills, and there they became the various Italian tribes. Most important of these to

39

our story were the Latins. For reasons of safety, these Latins, like the others, lived in the craggiest places they could find, but they always came down to the *campania,* as the level land was called, to fatten their lowing herds. And in 754 B.C., according to Roman legend, twin brothers, Romulus and Remus, decided to stay there. They became chieftains of a band of robber cattle-herders, and at the exact spot where the twins said they had been nourished as babes by a she-wolf (who some say was a woman named Lupa, the Latin word for "wolf"), they founded a small town of mud-and-wattle houses.

They named it Rome after Romulus, the older twin. Little did anyone dream that one day it would be one of the most famous cities in the world! Still less did anyone imagine that the Romans would march out of it to conquer the world!

But that is just exactly what they did. In the beginning, they had troubles and trials. In fact, an old story says that when the Gauls from France invaded the city, the capital was saved only when a gaggle of geese cackled and warned the senators.

But the Romans were stubborn, good fighters, well-disciplined, and no matter how bitterly they battled each other in more than one bloody civil war, they always stood together when they faced an enemy. By the time of Julius Caesar 700 years later, they had reached the English Channel in one direction and the Caspian Sea in the other. When Trajan was emperor (about 100 A.D.), practically every part of the known civilized world was included in their empire. Of the eighty-two countries in the United Nations at the time this book was written, all or a part of at least thirty were in Trajan's empire, and a great majority of the other fifty-two countries are in lands, like America, that hadn't been discovered. They were ruled by one man.

What is more, soon all the inhabitants of all these lands were Roman citizens. *Civis Romanus sum.* I am a Roman citizen. This could be said by longhaired Celts walking the heather in Britain; by Berbers in the Atlas Mountains in Africa; by haughty Spaniards (Trajan himself was born in Spain); by Gauls in France, Egyptians, Greeks, Syrians, Arabs; even by Scythians and Sarmatians from South Russia, and by Germans from across the Rhine.

This was a great achievement that had never happened before, but it also made a lot of difficulties.

Take size alone. The Roman Empire was now too big to manage. In those days, you couldn't fly a general (or a tax collector, or an imperial officer, or the emperor himself) from York, England—that's where Constantine the Great was when he started toward Rome to become the Roman emperor —to the Persian border in a matter of hours. You couldn't even put him on a fast train. The Roman roads were famous, but the only way you could travel them was on foot, on horseback, or in a litter or chariot. And from one end of the empire to the other was 3,000 miles!

Two centuries after Trajan, an emperor called Diocletian decided to do something about it. Diocletian was the son of a freed slave, but he became the first absolute ruler the Roman Empire ever had. Before that the emperor was merely *princeps* (from which the English word "prince" is derived), or first citizen. But once Diocletian had all this power, he proceeded to divide it up. He appointed a co-emperor (a second Augustus) with an assistant emperor called a *caesar* to help him, and put him in charge of the Roman Empire in the West.

Diocletian himself, with his own *caesar,* kept the East. Although he was still head emperor and the other emperor was supposed to obey him, the Roman Empire was now divided into two parts.

About forty years later, another emperor took an even more important step. Constantine the Great decided that the empire needed a second capital as much as it needed two rulers, and since he was a Christian emperor—actually he was the first Christian emperor—he decided it must be a Christian city.

He looked around him carefully. First he thought of Nicomedia (now Ismid in modern Turkey) where Diocletian had had his camp; but it had been the capital of a heathen king. Then he considered ancient Troy, for the Romans were supposed to be descended from the Trojans. He even began to build walls there. But one day somebody reminded him of the ruined city of Byzantium with its wonderful location.

"That is the place!" he cried.

On foot, with lance in hand and followed by a solemn procession, he marched over pleasant hills and valleys that were still covered with vines and greenery.

As they tried to keep up with him his panting courtiers asked him how big he planned to make the place.

"I shall walk," he replied, "until God, my invisible Guide, bids me to halt."

An emperor could get things done in those days. Not much more than four years from the day, hour, and minute that Constantine ordered his architects and engineers and builders to get to work, the city was completed and ready to live in. It was equipped with theaters, public baths, senate houses, a university, courts of justice, granaries, palaces, and magnificent private dwellings, many of them the very ones described by Robert of Clari. It had broad squares, paved avenues, classic porticoes, and aqueducts that brimmed with clear, cool water. It was decorated with marbles, statues, and priceless works of art; at the emperor's command, the cities of Greece and Asia Minor had been rifled of their most precious treasures to make sure of this.

It was filled with people too. Constantine invited (that was the same thing as *ordered*) senators to move from Rome. He presented costly buildings to his favorites. He confiscated the estates of many of his rich subjects, especially in Asia Minor, and gave the income to those of his subjects who agreed to live in the new city. Of course, a lot of people came of their own accord. They wanted to get in on something good.

It was lucky indeed that Diocletian and Constantine had taken these steps. For suddenly the Roman Empire began to quake and tremble. All through recorded history and long before, the barbarians from the northern swamps and forests of Europe kept pouring down upon the lands to the south of them. As a matter of fact, the Romans, as well as the Greeks whom Homer wrote his poems about, were from the north. When Homer spoke of the "golden-haired Achaeans," he was talking about the Greeks. But the men around the Mediterranean—the original Greeks—were dark, as they are today. The Achaeans came from the north.

For a long time Roman might had kept these tribesmen back, and civilization and a comfortable life had flourished. As many men lived in peace or happiness as ever have before or since.

But now all at once Rome grew weak almost as fast as it had grown powerful, and the barbarians rode again. Almost immediately they were able to cross the frontiers whenever they wanted to. Soon the empire couldn't hold them off at all.

Less than a century after Constantine, Alaric the Goth marched into Rome and burned a great deal of the city. Forty-five years later another tribe, the Vandals, destroyed the rest. We get the word "vandalism" from the Vandals. It means the willful destruction of something beautiful, which is what the Vandals did. After the Vandals other Germanic tribes, with their horned helmets and their long yellow hair, came streaming in, bringing their women and children with them. They were followed by the Mongolian Huns and Avars.

In 476 A.D., one of the barbarian chiefs decided it was foolish to pretend any longer. He deposed the then Roman emperor, Romulus Augustulus (a Latin name meaning "Romulus, the little Augustus"), and proclaimed himself king of Italy. Thus ended the Roman Empire in the West.

If it had not been for Diocletian and Constantine, it would also have ended the Roman Empire everywhere. It might have ended Western civilization, too.

But the emperor of the Roman Empire in the East stood safe behind his mighty walls, and he announced as quickly as possible that he was now emperor of the whole Roman Empire. He ordered this barbarian king of Italy and all the other barbarian kings to acknowledge him as emperor and overlord.

Many of them did.

That is probably the most important thing to remember about the Byzantines. They considered themselves Romans. Most people in the West called them Greeks, and indeed they spoke Greek and were Greek in many other ways. They were also Orientals in their splendor. But for at least the first 900 years of their history they thought of themselves as Romans and were proud of it. Their emperor was still the Augustus, and his other title *autokrator* was a Greek translation of the

Latin *imperator*, or commander in chief. Even when he later took the proud title of *basileus*, a Greek equivalent for the Persian "king of kings," he was *basileus ton Romaion*, king of the Romans. To call him "Greek emperor," as did some Westerners, was to use a fighting word.

The second most important thing to remember about the Byzantines was that Constantinople never fell into the hands of the enemy. This means that the empire never fell into the hands of the barbarians, for in those days the capital was even more important than it is today, and so in spite of all the lands it governed, Constantinople *was* the empire. As long as it stood, the empire stood. The Byzantines had plenty of troubles, and more than once saw the turbans and scimitars of the Arabs, and the felt hats and yellow faces of the followers of some steppe-riding khagan, right beneath their walls. But except when he was invited, no foreign invader had ever set foot in the streets of Constantinople until Geoffrey of Villehardouin and Robert of Clari came with their fellow crusaders.

It is a fact that for century after century, when almost every other important city in the world was sacked and looted over and over again, the Byzantines were able to make and keep Constantinople safe. It was a place of refuge for men and for ideas and for the civilization the Greeks and Romans had given them and for the ideals of Christianity in the midst of a stormy world.

ThE holY AuGusTus

The Byzantines were able to keep Constantinople safe because they were one of the few peoples living in the time between the fall of Rome and modern days who had a strong government and one that worked. The rest of the Roman Empire had been divided by conquest into a good hundred or more independent units. These were ruled by kings, princes, dukes, marquises, and counts, and some cities were even free republics headed by wrangling priors. Their boundaries were always changing, and nobody ever knew just who was governing whom today, and who would be tomorrow. But the eastern half of the Roman Empire had a single government which was almost always orderly.

The Byzantines were able to do it because they had a fine army, and when they needed it, a swift and deadly navy—to

46

say nothing of a diplomatic corps with a well-paid staff of skillful, highly trained diplomats.

They were able to do it because of their Christianity. After Antioch (in Syria) and Alexandria (in Egypt) had been captured by the Arabs, Constantinople was the most important Christian city except Rome. And as far as the Byzantines were concerned, the state worked for Christianity, and Christianity worked for the state.

Finally, the Byzantine Empire was able to stand firm and to last so long because the Byzantines could afford to spend what they needed to. Their government was tremendously expensive. Their army and their navy with its *strategoi* and *drungariuses* (generals and admirals) cost them a lot of money and so did their extravagant ambassadors. The church with its own mighty army of high officials and lesser functionaries was very expensive too.

But as long as the Byzantines were not only able to support emperor, army, navy, diplomats, and the church, but were *willing* to do so, the Byzantine Empire flourished and was great. It was only after they began to economize, when a lot of Byzantines decided they were spending too much on the army, that their troubles began.

At the head of the government was the emperor, and he was certainly the most absolute ruler there could possibly be. Even in the earliest days of the empire, he was chief of the Byzantine state, commander in chief of the army and navy, the only one who could make laws, and the head of the Byzantine courts. In other words, he was equivalent to the President, Congress, and the Supreme Court of the United States rolled into one.

When he became *basileus,* he was even more than that. The Great King was master and owner as well as sovereign, and his subjects became slaves. They had to humble themselves on the ground before him, and foreigners had to as well. Beside that, he was the head of the Byzantine church (now known as the Greek, or Orthodox Eastern, Church), and in this connection took on another title, *isapostolos*, which is Greek for "equal to the Apostles."

But in spite of his great power, in many ways he was a democratic emperor who was elected or at least chosen by a process carefully set down by law. First he had to be named by either the senate or the army. Then he had to be approved by whichever of those two bodies that had not named him in the first place. Finally he had to be hailed by the people. (This was true even when the emperor seized power or when an emperor named his son co-emperor so that he would be sure to succeed him. He still had to be approved and hailed.) But once the emperor was elected, he was "the emperor chosen by God," for the Byzantines firmly believed that God guided them in everything they did. From then on, it was not only treason but wicked and sinful to oppose the emperor. That is, unless you were successful. If you led a successful revolution, it meant that God had chosen you to take the old emperor's place!

The empress—the Augusta, or *basilissa*, as she was also called—was almost equally important. To be sure, in the long history of the Byzantine Empire, only three women actually mounted the throne to rule in their own name, and only one of these amounted to anything. This was the wicked Irene who wanted to marry Charlemagne and who blinded her own son so she could stay in power. However, she did not call herself empress. She called herself emperor of the Romans just as if she had been a man.

But even though she rarely ruled, the empress was not shut

up in a harem, and many empresses had great power and even greater influence.

Ariadne, the widow of an early emperor, went before the people and told them that her husband was dead. "Choose us a new ruler!" they clamored. She named a palace official, and then she married him. He was a very good ruler.

Zoe, the daughter of another emperor, did even better. She married three men, and each in turn became emperor.

More than that. The nephew of her second husband persuaded her to adopt him and name him her co-emperor. Then he had her hair shorn and shipped her off to the Princes Islands, in the Sea of Marmara, as a nun.

The crowds surged around the palace. "Where is our lovely lady," they shouted, "whose father, grandfather, and great-grandfather ruled before her?" The usurper had to bring her back, but even that did not save him. He ended in a monastery himself.

Saint Theodora (the wife of an emperor and the mother of one) used her influence to end a religious dispute that had disturbed the state for more than 100 years, while another Theodora, who was far from a saint, saved it from revolution.

This happened when the Greens and the Blues (the rival political parties) joined forces and revolted against Justinian, the greatest Byzantine emperor of all. After they had burned much of the city, they surged into the Circus and called on the emperor to abdicate.

The mighty Justinian, who had even ordered a ship ready for a quick escape, was about to give in when suddenly his empress, Theodora, stood beside him. She was an ex-circus girl, one of the people herself.

"You can do what you want to," she told him, her eyes flashing. "I am going to stay here. Anyone who puts on the crown must never take it off. If I die, I am going to be buried in imperial purple!"

The emperor was ashamed of himself.

"Drive them back to their warrens!" he ordered two of his toughest generals.

Within hours, the riots were put down.

But even when the empress did not do things like this, she was very important. For this reason a widower emperor remarried as soon as possible. Leo the Philosopher married four times and got into almost as much trouble as Henry VIII. If an emperor didn't remarry, he made his daughter the Augusta.

"When there is not an Augusta," wrote a Byzantine, "it is not possible to celebrate holidays or give banquets or entertainments in the manner prescribed by law."

That may not seem important to us, but it was very important to the Byzantines. Since the emperor was God's representative on earth, every official act of his life had to be like a church service, and in almost every one of the more than eighty occasions described in detail in an instruction book for emperors called *The Book of Ceremonies*, the empress took part.

It was something to see the royal pair on any great Byzantine holiday, for example, May 11, when they celebrated the founding of the city.

On this day the statue of Constantine the Great was paraded through the city in a golden chariot drawn by white mules, and the emperor sat in the Hippodrome waiting to pay honor to it. He was clad in robes that literally glittered. His principal garment was a tunic which reached almost to his ankles. This was called the *scaramangion* and was so stiff with brocade that it could have stood by itself. Over this was a shorter garment called the *saigon*. It was purple, gold-embroidered, and seeded with pearls. On his head he wore the *stemmata*, or imperial crown. It twinkled with rubies and sapphires of the purest ray serene. On his feet were the *campagia*, or special boots that only the emperor could wear. These too were of imperial purple, although some people say this imperial purple was really a deep crimsony red.

The empress sat at his side, just as splendid as he. Her garments were much like his, but on her crown was a plume made of precious stones. She wore earrings that dangled far below her shoulders, and sometimes a neckpiece made of oval or pear-shaped pearls. If he was a solid gold emperor, she was a solid gold empress too.

Yet in spite of all the splendor and glory (and this is only a little bit of it), the Byzantine emperor did not have to be royally born. In the Byzantine Empire it was just as easy to rise from a hovel to the throne as it is to be born in humble circumstances and become President of the United States.

Many of the emperors did.

An early emperor had been a butcher. Another had been a swineherd from Macedonia, and the great Justinian was this swineherd's nephew. The savage Phocas was originally a centurion (a top sergeant). Still another had once been a donkey trader who moved from one country fair to another. Basil I was raised as a Balkan farm boy. He was very tall and strong and attracted the attention of the reigning emperor because he could tame horses. A later emperor had been a petty officer in the navy. Still another was originally a dockyard worker.

Many of the empresses were humbly born too. Besides Theodora, the circus girl, there was one who had been a cook, and a third who was the daughter of a saloonkeeper. Even

Saint Theodora was brought up in poverty because her father, who had once been a courtier, had given all his money to the poor.

Saint Theodora became empress when the emperor picked his bride by following an old custom of the Byzantine emperors. Wishing to marry, he sent messengers throughout his realm, telling them to bring back the most beautiful young women they could find. Seventeen were paraded before him, and when the one he was about to choose annoyed him by a flippant answer she made, he chose Theodora.

Theodora did not intend to stay poor like her father. One day, her husband, the emperor, looked out of the window and saw a rich, heavily laden merchant vessel sail in and tie up to a wharf.

"I wonder who owns it," he mused.

"It is mine," said the empress.

The emperor flew into a fury. *His* wife should not be engaged in trade like some huckster. He made her sell it, but he did let her keep the profits.

Because these rulers were the emperors chosen by God, the Byzantines bowed their knee to them as the ancient Egyptians had to the Pharaohs. But because they were from the people, and also because the Byzantines had sharp tongues and liked to be sarcastic, the people sometimes gave their rulers a rough time.

There were more than 100 emperors in the long period of the Byzantine Empire, and many of them were given nicknames. Some of these nicknames were far from flattering.

Here are just a few: Justinian Nose-Cut-Off. (This was Justinian II, not the great Justinian.) Constantine the Stable Boy. Michael the Stutterer. Michael the Drunkard. Constantine Born-in-the-Purple. Basil the Bulgar Slayer. Michael Thinks-He's-a-Soldier. Even one empress had a nickname; Leo the Philosopher's fourth wife was called Zoe Black Eyes.

The emperors had to put up with sarcastic epigrams, disrespectful poems, and uncomplimentary stories. Here is one of them: Michael Thinks-He's-a-Soldier had a passion for city planning, but he hated to spend money. One day the Byzantines saw a principal avenue all torn up. The pavement had been removed and workmen were everywhere.

"What is happening?" asked one of them. "Oh, yes! I remember! That's where the emperor lost one of his halfpenny dice when he was a small boy. He's tearing up the pavement to find it!"

But in spite of all this, or maybe because of it, the Byzantine state was about as solid as was possible. Not even revolutions could really shake it.

One reason may have been the fact that since the emperors came from every class and were often changing, the Byzantines were constantly getting new and vigorous blood in their government. But another reason was the wonderful and well-organized body of bureaucrats who helped the emperor govern the empire. When there was a strong emperor, these men carried out his orders. When there was a weak emperor, they did the best they could, until a new, strong emperor mounted the throne.

There was really nothing like this group in any other government in the world until modern times. They were trained public servants, headed by high officials who were appointed by the emperor.

The most important of these officials was the Logothete of the Dromos. (The word *logothete* really means accountant, but it is like a secretary in the United States Cabinet.) He was also known as the Grand Logothete. He was secretary of state, minister of police, and secretary of the interior.

Besides that, there was a Logothete of the Treasury who was like the Secretary of the Treasury of the United States; a Logothete of the Military Chest, who was the paymaster general of the army and navy; and a Logothete of the Flocks and Herds who was in charge of all the vast imperial estates. Among other things, he ran the imperial horse farms where practically all the horses needed by the empire and the army were raised.

There was also the Sacellerius, or Controller General; the Quaestor, or Minister of Justice; the Grand Domestic, or commander in chief of the army; and the Grand Drungarius, or secretary of the navy. These are only a few of the most important officials.

Under these department heads—and even more important —were the humble clerks who really did the work of government. These clerks were banded together into a body called the *logothesia* which was almost like our modern civil service. They were well paid, and even the lowest-ranking workers had unlimited opportunities for graft. In those days, graft was not considered dishonest; it was more like the tip that you give to a waiter for his service.

The clerks were also rewarded with honors. Every Byzantine working for the government had two titles. One described his job, such as chief clerk to the third assistant to the *eparch,* or lord mayor of Constantinople. The other was the rank given to him to recognize his services. Around the emperor alone there were twenty-six ranks, ranging in order of importance from *caesar* down to *nipsistarios,* a man who sprinkled symbolic holy water on the sovereign. In the city and throughout the empire were sixty other ranks. The badge that was the symbol of each of these was as important to a Byzantine as his pay.

It was this government, and most of all its lower-rank employees, that really ran the Byzantine Empire, for nobody could get on without them. Emperors and even logothetes came and went, but the Byzantine civil service clerks were always there. If an army had to be sent to an overseas province, the clerks knew how many ships and how much time it would take to get there. If there was a famine, they knew how many bushels of wheat were needed to feed Constantinople, and where to get them.

They were for the most part plain citizens from all over the

Byzantine state who had come to the capital not to get rich but just to make a living. They were noisy. They liked to argue. They were quarrelsome and jealous. As they jostled through the crowded streets toward their homes or pushed their way onto the crowded Mesé to buy silk for their wives or food for their larder, they reeked of garlic and highly spiced fish. But they kept the empire alive.

A ROMAN ARMY ON HORSEBACK

The army kept the empire going too.

It called itself the Roman army; and this Roman army of the Greek Byzantine Empire was about as efficient as any body of armed men between the time of Julius Caesar and the days of gunpowder and artillery.

Actually, though, Julius Caesar would have been astonished if he had seen it. Who, he would have asked, were these swarthy-skinned, black-bearded men with their quick and glinting Asiatic eyes? The commands seemed to be given in Latin, but the accent made them hard to understand. Why were so many of them on prancing, spirited horses?

Caesar would have remembered his legions like the famous Tenth Legion with which he landed in Britain. Rome had conquered the world with her legions. The legion was a body of from 4,000 to 6,000 citizen-soldiers. Except for a small handful who were mounted for scouting, the legion was made up entirely of foot soldiers. The tough men who fought in its ranks were clean-shaven, and each one carried a large shield. He wore a round helmet and a leather cuirass, and was armed with a short Spanish thrusting sword (that is, you didn't hack with it) and a short throwing spear called a *pilum*.

But when in 378 A.D., a mighty Roman emperor was surrounded and crushed by barbarian horsemen in a Balkan valley not more than 150 miles from Constantinople, the infantry and the legion did not look unbeatable any more.

The Byzantines decided not to rely on it.

So first Caesar would have seen a large array of well-equipped men on sturdy chargers. These were the heavy cavalry, later known as *cataphracts*. They were as renowned as any Byzantine troops. They wore steel caps, and on each cap was a crest showing the colors of that *bandon*, or horse regiment. They also wore long mail shirts, steel gauntlets, steel shoes, and sometimes a light surcoat. Even the horses, at least those of the officers and the men in the front rank, had steel head armor and breastplates. For weapons, each man had a broadsword, a dagger, a bow and a quiver of arrows, and a long lance with a banderole, also in the *bandon* colors. They could charge like knights, or by acting as bowmen, they could fight a distant enemy.

Then Caesar would have seen the light troopers, or *trapezidae*. These too were cavalry, but they were the light cavalry. They did carry shields, but for body armor they wore only a cuirass of very light mail or horn. For weapons, they had only a lance and a sword.

There was still infantry in the Byzantine army, but it was now pretty unimportant. It was used mostly for holding ground which the cavalry had won. But even the infantry was divided into two groups. The heavy infantry were about as well armored as the *cataphracts*. For weapons, they carried a short, heavy battle ax and a dagger. They could stand off a barbarian cavalry charge. The light infantry wore no armor, but carried long-range bows. The Byzantine method of fighting was something like the German blitzkrieg, with cavalry taking the place of swiftly moving tanks and the foot soldiers following behind.

The Byzantines did much more than change their army into something swift and moving, however. They did more than divide the old clumsy legion into smaller units almost like our modern regiments, battalions, companies, and platoons. They spent a lot of time thinking about the whole business of fighting and may even have been the inventors of carefully planned strategy. They would not have been at all surprised at our modern war colleges where even generals are taught in the classroom what to do on the field of battle.

As a matter of fact, at least three Byzantine emperors wrote very good books on the art of war. These books included much more than just how to equip and drill an army. They also told the general exactly how he should fight his battles, and they emphasized that he must have a different kind of warfare for each different kind of foe.

The Franks, for example—and by the Franks, the Byzantines meant German and north Italian peoples quite as much as French and Normans—believe, said the books, that a retreat under any circumstances is dishonorable. Better die than show your back to the enemy. They are also very careless about outposts and scouts. So if you are fighting the Franks, you should try to trap them in a place where they will be at a disadvantage. Then you can annihilate them.

With the Turks—and by the Turks, the Byzantines also

meant the Hungarians, the Patzinaks, and all the people of
the Asiatic steppes—it is another matter, the books continued.
They are light horsemen who carry bow and arrow as well
as javelin and scimitar. They are hard to surprise because they
always post mounted sentinels. Also you must be careful if
you pursue them, for they don't stay defeated but rally
quickly. However, the heavy Byzantine *cataphracts* can ride
them down and cut them to pieces. They are supposed to do
so. And the Turks do not dare attack the Byzantine infantry
because of its strong and powerful bows.

The Slavs, on the other hand, are only dangerous when they
are led by Bulgarian khagans or by viking princes, and even
then they are only really dangerous when they are in the hills.
The thing to do, said the strategy books, is to lure them to the
plains in hope of plunder. And then destroy them.

But the really difficult enemy faced by the Byzantines were
the newly risen Arabs, or Saracens.

These wild sheiks from the desert were fanatically brave,
for Mohammed had taught them that the easiest way to get to
heaven was to die killing the unbeliever. Their numbers were
limitless, for after they had conquered Egypt and Syria they
drew into their ranks every discontented person in the Middle
East. Once a year they poured, like a horde of locusts, through
the gates of the Taurus Mountains into what today is southern Turkey. Nothing, including the Byzantine army, could
stop them.

But fortunately, if they were wild and brave, they were also
greedy for plunder, and besides that they could not stand cold
or rain. So once a year too, usually in October or November,
they turned back again, and their mules and camels, loaded
down with booty, could not move back as fast as they had
come.

"This is the way to beat them," said one of the strategy books. "Always know where they are. Whether you are eating, taking a bath or sleeping, never turn away a man who says that he has information. Whether he is a freeman or a slave—no matter who he is!"

And then track them down, catching them in the narrow, snowy, chilly mountain passes if possible. They won't fight well when they are trapped and shivering. Or if they don't go back of their own accord, raid their own country and in this way bait them back. But whenever you fight them, or anyone else, be sure you know what you are doing. Above all, don't throw everything into the battle at once. The general with the last reserves always wins.

The Byzantines also taught their generals not only how to fight but when to fight, and also when not to fight, which was even more important. They believed that it was better to be safe than sorry. The Byzantine general was told that he must never be rash, and above everything he must never throw his troops into battle where they might be killed or wounded if he could win the day by stratagems or tricks.

To be sure, he must always keep his pledged word. If he didn't, who would believe him next time? And the lives of captives must always be spared if possible. One day they might be on the Byzantine side.

But it was all right to send an officer under a flag of truce and have him pretend that he wanted to discuss terms for surrender, when he was really acting as a spy. In the meantime, the Byzantines could bring up reinforcements. It was all right to forge letters showing that an enemy commander was turning traitor and then arrange to have them fall into his general's hands. It was all right to disguise soldiers as innocent herdsmen driving bleating sheep and lowing cattle, and have them lure the enemy into a prepared ambush. Obviously, a feigned retreat was a recognized part of the game. Even a real retreat did not disgrace a Byzantine general, although the Byzantines were just as brave and proud as anyone else. At least the general who retreated would have some soldiers left and could fight and win another day.

The Byzantines also believed that if you wanted a good army, you must pay it well and treat it even better. A general's salary could be as much as forty pounds of gold a year, and even a recruit had cash in his pocket. When a soldier served his time he might also get a grant of land. There was a well-organized supply department, and the soldiers were always sure of beans, cheese, and wine, to say nothing of what they could plunder from the country. A special corps of engineers pitched their tents for them and set up huge baths. The soldiers were even allowed to have slaves and servants. The army itself provided a groom for every four cavalrymen, and every sixteen foot soldiers had an attendant who drove a cart carrying all they needed. There was even an ambulance corps of stretcher bearers and surgeons. The stretcher bearers were paid a gold coin for every wounded man they brought from the field.

This is what the Byzantine regular army was like, but besides that, especially in the early days, there were regiments or even whole tribes of Huns, Goths, Alans, and other barbarians who fought for the emperor under their own chieftains. Later on, particularly in Asia Minor, there were also the great feudal lords, or Border Men.

There is a wonderful Byzantine poem called *Digenes Akrites* about one of these men. Its hero is Basil Digenes Akrites, son of an Arab emir named Monsour and a Greek lady of the noble Dukas family. For this reason he is called Digenes Akrites, which means "border man of two races."

Basil was a valiant knight like Roland and Sir Lancelot, and in spite of his Arab father, he was a faithful Christian. And so when he wasn't slaying lions, fighting cattle thieves, or rescuing lovely damsels, he was ready to join forces with the emperor and lead his men against the infidel.

But he only did this when he thought the emperor was right! When one of the emperors came to visit his castle he was quite willing to give him a lecture on how an emperor should act.

Both the barbarians, with their hard-riding horsemen, and the valiant border lords played an important part in defending the Byzantine Empire from its enemies, but the Byzantines never really trusted either group. A barbarian chieftain was far too likely to ride off with his hordes and found a kingdom of his own as Theodoric had done in Italy. A border lord from Asia Minor was too likely to try to become emperor himself. Indeed, more than one had.

The Byzantines also had a navy, one of the best navies of the Middle Ages. But often they did not rely on it as they did on their army. For one thing, the emperors were always afraid of the navy for the same reason that they were afraid of the border lords of Asia. They were fearful that some admiral would use it to take their throne from them. Three admirals did just that. Another reason was that the Byzantines liked to be sure of what they were doing. But in those days, ships were flimsy and the seas were full of unknown rocks and sudden storms. The best of plans might be upset by the violence of nature, and so it was more dependable to fight on land.

Just the same, when the Byzantines had to, they were always able to get together a fleet, and it was usually a good one. When Justinian sent an invasion army to North Africa, he had enough ships to need 20,000 sailors. It was the navy that twice drove the Arabs from Constantinople. In 853 A.D., the Byzantines were able to send 300 ships against Egypt. A little later, Zoe Black Eyes could order a veritable armada all the way to Italy to drive Saracen sea raiders from their stronghold near Naples. When the Byzantines attacked the pirates in Crete, they were able to send 105 dromonds and 75 Pamphylians. The dromond was the battleship of the Middle Ages. It sometimes carried 300 men and was a bireme, that is, it had two decks of oars on each side, one under the other. A Pamphylian was a lighter, swifter cruiser. The admiral's flagship was usually a Pamphylian. There were also galleys; they had only one bank of oars but were the swiftest of all.

It was the Byzantine navy that developed and used what was probably the first "secret weapon" of all history. This was the famous Greek fire. Even today nobody knows exactly what it was, except that it was a complicated mixture of chemicals, one of which may have been a crude form of petroleum.

The Byzantines pumped it at the enemy through huge tubes or hurled it at them from portable siphons almost like modern flame throwers. Even water would not put it out. So it was fairly easy to destroy an enemy fleet. Greek fire frightened the enemy even more.

But the Byzantines did not rely only on the army or the navy to win their battles for them. Helping them in every way was the Byzantine diplomatic service. For just as the Byzantines did not ever fight a battle if they could find some other way of winning it, so too they didn't even begin a war unless they had to. Why fight if they could persuade an enemy to become their friend and ally? Why fight, and risk their own safety, if they could talk someone else into fighting for them? To the Byzantines, this made sense.

It was up to their diplomatic service to do this, and the reason it was able to do so very often was because here too the Byzantines knew just what they were doing. Under the Logothete of the Dromos, they had an almost modern intelligence system taken care of by a special department whose one job was to collect information about foreign nations.

How can such and such a country help the Byzantines and how can it hurt them?

How can it best be won over by the Byzantines—by force, by honors and favors, or by gifts?

If the last, by what kind of gifts?

Has it any enemies, and if so, who are they?

What were its origins? What is its history? What is its climate and its geographical position?

Has it usually been a friend or an enemy of the Byzantines? Trace this back to the day when it first appeared on the scene!

With this information—the questions had been carefully worked out by the emperor Constantine Born-in-the-Purple in a book called *How To Run the Empire*—the Byzantines could select the right method for the nation they were interested in and then go to work on it.

If the ruler or his ambassador was easily dazzled, they could impress him with court ceremony and with purple shoes and robes, and they might even give out a title or two such as patrician or *archon*. They might even take some northern duke or count and promote him to be prince or king provided he swore allegiance to them.

If he was greedy and avaricious—and, said Constantine, "the tribes of the north demand everything and hanker after everything"—they could give him cash in hand or even pay an annual tribute.

As a last resort, the emperor could marry a foreign princess or give a sister or a daughter in marriage to a foreign prince. The Byzantines did not really approve of the latter, especially the ladies who were shipped off to some outlandish country without Byzantine comforts or conveniences! "I am being sacrificed to the wild beast of the West!" wailed one of them. But it often worked wonders. From distant Asbagia under the towering snow-crowned Caucasus Mountains to distant Germany, where the "wild beast of the West" lived, many and many a kingdom was made friendly to the Byzantines because a Byzantine princess sat on its throne.

But of course when an emperor did this, he must never give the barbarians all they asked for, and he must always think up a good reason for not doing so. If they asked for an imperial crown or an imperial robe, he must point out that these were sacred and consecrated and tell of the horrendous death suffered by one emperor who had given some to his Khazar relatives. If they asked for Greek fire, he must tell them that it was given by an angel and that anyone who gave it away would be struck down from heaven. If they sought to marry a princess, he must tell them that the demand is monstrous, even though the royal robe-makers were already embroidering the wedding gown.

In that way he would not only save some of his valuable possessions, but the barbarians would appreciate the ones he did give them all the more.

ONE RELIGION, ONE CHURCH

Last of the things that made the Byzantine Empire strong and powerful was the Byzantine church. In some ways, it was the most important of all.

The Byzantine Empire was much more than just one half of the old Roman Empire dragging out its days for another thousand years. It was a new Roman Empire based on Christianity. Practically every Byzantine was a Christian, and so it was Christianity that united all the many races and languages into a single people. In spite of all the arguments about this doctrine and that doctrine, practically every Byzantine believed in the official Orthodox faith, and as the emperor was head of this faith, that gave him additional power.

Even a weak emperor could point to the Bible. "Render therefore unto Caesar the things which are Caesar's; and unto God the things that are God's." But the emperor was *caesar*, and he was God's representative too. He had to be obeyed on both counts.

The Byzantines were by nature an intensely religious people. They were Middle Easterners as well as Greek, and more than half of the world's great religions were born in the Middle East—Judaism, Christianity, and Islam, to name just the most important three.

The Byzantines had been religious from the very beginning, and the Greek side of their nature made them like to talk and argue about their religion as well.

Saint Gregory of Nyssa visited Constantinople when it was only forty years old, and even this holy man threw up his hands in astonishment. The money changer who converted his Asiatic money into Byzantine gold, the white-faced baker who sold him a loaf of bread, even the slave boy who mixed hot and cold water for him at the public bath, all wanted to discuss the fine points of Christian beliefs with him.

Saint Gregory shook his head. "Everybody in this city seems to be a doctor of theology," he said. "*Everybody!* Even the slaves and day laborers. There isn't a man in the city who can't preach a good sermon, and they all do if you give them half a chance. If you don't believe me, just stand at any street corner! Just go into any shop!"

But it was not merely the servants and shopkeepers who were deeply wrapped up in religion. High or low, virtually every Byzantine, even including those who spent most of their time making money and amassing worldly goods, had been taught from childhood and absolutely believed that life in this world was a vain shadow and the important thing was to win everlasting bliss in heaven. But this could only be done through religion and the church.

That may have been why many rich Byzantines and even

many a Byzantine emperor or empress liked to endow monasteries, just as in modern times many rich men set up foundations. In fact, so many monasteries were set up in this way that it became necessary to pass a law stating that if you wanted to found a monastery, you must sell the land and only give the money. Many of the greatest estates were being left to the church and since they then didn't have to pay taxes any more, it grew more and more difficult for the state to raise all the money it needed.

Many Byzantines, including emperors, became monks before they died. They felt more sure of their reward in the future if they actually entered a monastery, had their heads shaven, and exchanged their golden garments for a hair shirt or a cowl.

That may also have been why so many patriarchs—the title of the head of the Byzantine church—did not fear the emperor, even though the emperor had appointed them.

One patriarch boldly told an emperor that no one had to obey his laws if they went against the church. The emperor exiled him but did not dare to harm him.

Another went even further.

"I made you emperor, you ignorant fool!" he shouted at Isaac Comnenus. "I can bring you down as easily."

He even put on the imperial purple shoes, saying the patriarch had a right to wear them. Of course, he didn't get away with this, but at least he had tried.

Sometimes, to be sure, Byzantine religion was very close to superstition, particularly among women and children.

You could make yourself a saint by becoming a stylite like Saint Simeon Stylites, who lived most of his life on top of a column sixty feet high without ever coming down. Simeon was venerated and even prayed to.

Many Byzantines were certain that cures could be effected by touching the arms, legs, and even the congealed sweat of some holy man. On the other hand, a doctor was howled down by the mob when he suggested ending a plague by letting fresh air into the crowded tenements.

"Blasphemy!" cried the Byzantines. "God decides when a man shall die, not fresh air!" When the doctor persisted, and died himself, they said God had punished him.

Others believed that cities had been saved by the apparition of some saint as much as by soldiers. For instance, when the Goths stormed toward Thessalonica (modern Salonika), the second city of the empire, Saint Demetrius appeared and led the East Roman army to victory. When the Avars reached Constantinople, the khagan saw a majestic female figure pacing the walls. It was the Theotokos, the Greek word for "Mother of God," which the Byzantines called the Virgin Mary. He turned back in panic.

Almost all the Byzantines paid great attention to fortune-telling, palm reading, and prophecies. Everybody believed in them. There were even more than a few emperors of humble birth who would not have even dared to try seizing the throne if it had not been for a fortuneteller or a prophecy. But, although sometimes the monks and abbots themselves told some of these fortunes, none of this had much to do with the church.

The Byzantine, even the most superstitious Byzantine, was truly Christian, but that did not mean he tolerated every kind of Christianity in existence. The Byzantine did not believe, as most of us do, that religion is a personal matter and that every man has a right to worship God in his own way, according to his own conscience. To the Byzantine, there was only one religion—the official religion. And there was only one church—his own Orthodox Church. If you believed anything else, you were a heretic and to be persecuted or fought.

This had been so from the very beginning. Constantine himself had called council after council to work out the details of the Christian creed, and the emperors who followed carried on his work. In council after council, they wrote down in black and white what every Byzantine had to believe. When it was written down, that was *it*. No further discussion about it, unless you enjoyed exile or having insulting poetry branded on your forehead; and this last really happened to one poor monk who refused to conform.

It was still true in the last days of the empire, but by then not even the emperor could change what had been agreed on earlier. Some of the later emperors tried to. They journeyed to France, Italy, and even England seeking help against the Turks, and in order to get the Western nations on their side they promised to make the Orthodox Church join the Roman Catholic Church, with the Pope as head of both.

The Byzantine people rose in protest. Lucas Notaras, a relative of the emperor and the last Megadux, or Great Admiral, shouted at his cousin angrily. "Better a Turkish turban than a papal miter!" he cried.

Although a huge Turkish cannon was already battering the walls, the mob shouted its approval.

"The Latins are trying to destroy the Greek city, the Greek religion, the Greek race, even the Greek language!" the people roared.

Even before there had been riots with the "democracy in rags," the poor people, joining the monks and abbots to make certain that the old-time religion of the Byzantines was kept true and pure even if this made the empire fall.

Nevertheless the old-time Orthodox Byzantine faith did not come into being just as it was and all at once. Since religion was so important, and since the Greeks loved to argue, the whole history of the Byzantines is filled with violent discussions and bitter differences of opinion about exactly what a man was supposed to believe. Some of the arguments were so complicated that it does not seem that the Byzantines themselves always understood them, even though they were willing to rush into the streets and fight about them. The arguments are even more hard to understand today.

One of the most bitter disputes was about the use of the single letter *i*. There is a Greek word *homoios* which means "similar," and another Greek word *homos* which means "same." Men and women were sent to distant sunless provinces or shipped to lonely islands; they were locked in damp, rat-infested cells; and volume after volume was written and published over whether the Saviour was *homoi-ousion* (similar to God) or *homo-ousion* (the same as God). But this was only one of many arguments and discussions. It would be impossible to tell you even a small part of them. But that does not mean that these differences were not important. Many people think that the reason the Arabs conquered Egypt and Syria so easily and converted the inhabitants to Islam was that most of the emperors were Orthodox Christians who tried to make the Egyptians and Syrians Orthodox, too.

The most important controversy that troubled the Byzantines is easier to understand. It is called the Iconoclast (image breaker) controversy, and it agitated the empire for more than a hundred years.

Although the early Christians had opposed images and paintings, calling them heathen idols, most Byzantines attached great importance to them. In fact, some of their finest art went into the making of statues, portraits, and even small portable mosaics of saints, apostles, and other holy persons. They called these *eikons,* and they certainly paid them great reverence. Their enemies said they even worshiped them.

But not every Byzantine was an image worshiper. The hardy mountaineers from Isauria and other parts of Asia Minor still held to the Puritan-like thoughts of their ancestors. They hated images. Then an Isaurian general seized the throne. In addition to hating images, he realized that image worship greatly increased the power of the monks and priests who were now just about as strong as the emperor.

Because they hated images, and also to break the power of the church party, he and his son and the other emperors who followed ordered every image to be torn down and many of them destroyed. Then they abolished many monasteries. In some cases they made the monks and nuns parade hand in hand before howling crowds in the Hippodrome, forcing them to choose between marriage or torture and death.

These Iconoclast emperors were supported by the soldiers (most of whom were also image breakers; and all wanted a chance to loot church treasures) and by much of Asia Minor. But the monks would not give in, many of them suffering martyrdom first, and *they* were supported by the people; by the superstitious sailors of the fleet; by all the women; and by many of the empresses who were as stubborn as the monks. Saint Theodora, for instance, although her husband was a strong Iconoclast, never gave up image worship in private and she taught her daughters and granddaughters to do the same. When she was surprised by a dwarf who told the emperor, she said that the figures they were praying to were really dolls and that she was playing with her grandchildren. But later she had the dwarf beaten for good measure.

With opposition like that, the Iconoclasts could not hope to win, and in the end they compromised. The images were restored, but they were to be placed high and out of reach. Worshipers could look at them or reverence them, but they could not kiss them or touch them.

It was at this time, and probably because harmony now reigned, that the Byzantine church at last felt powerful enough not only to take care of its own peoples' religion, but to set out to convert their heathen neighbors. Particularly their Slavic neighbors! Many of these still worshiped pagan gods 800 years after Christ.

It was Michael the Drunkard, a much better emperor than the name seems to indicate, who ended the Iconoclast controversy. And it was the same Michael who sent out Saint Cyril and Saint Methodius to do their work. They were the most famous missionaries eastern Europe had ever seen.

They prepared themselves like generals going into battle, and in a way they were like generals. They carefully restudied the Slavic languages, for since they were from a part of the empire where there were many Slavs, they already knew some Slavic languages. They learned all about Slavic culture and Slavic history. Finally they invented what is known today as the Cyrillic alphabet, which is still used in much of the Slavic world.

To be sure, their mission was not a complete success. They converted Moravia, now a part of Czechoslovakia, without too much difficulty, but when the Moravian king was defeated by a German king the country became Roman Catholic. Cyril and Methodius or saints trained by them, for they actually trained saints, went into Bulgaria, Macedonia, and Serbia. The people there stayed converted and stayed Orthodox. Indeed, Bulgaria soon boasted that it was the "eldest daughter of the eastern church," and had its own patriarch, and its own Santa Sophia, too.

But the most important conversion made by the Byzantines took place a hundred years later. It was the conversion of the Russians. The Russians themselves say this was done more by Byzantine splendor than by the talk of Byzantine missionaries, or even by the marriage of the Russian Prince Vladimir to the emperor's sister, Anna.

In 989, this huge ruler with his forest-shaking voice decided to make his people abandon their Norse gods and goddesses. He sent ambassadors to the four great religions that he knew about to find out which one was the best to adopt.

First the ambassadors went to the Black Bulgars, who were Moslems. But the mosques were smelly and dirty, and the Black Bulgars told the Russians that they would have to give up wine.

"Drinking is the joy of the Russians!" roared Vladimir.

Next they visited the Jewish Khazars, but how, asked Vladimir, could the Jews be God's chosen people if he had scattered them all over the earth?

Then they went to the German Roman Catholics.

"The Germans say that they worship the truth," the ambassadors reported, "but they have day after day of fasting, and there is no magnificence."

"I do not like to fast," said Vladimir.

Finally, they visited the Greeks, that is, the Byzantines.

"The Greeks," they said, "led us to the edifices where they worship their God, and we knew not whether we were in heaven or on earth, for nowhere have we seen such splendor and beauty. We are at loss how to describe it, but we do know that God must dwell there."

Then they added, "If the Greek faith was not good, your grandmother Olga would not have adopted it."

For they knew that this straw-haired princess had never stopped talking about the domes of polished copper, the pavements of rare stone, the magnificent decorations, the pearl-encrusted psalm books and Bibles, the incense and the music in Constantinople. They knew too that she had never stopped talking about the God-chosen emperor who had wanted to marry her, and how she had tricked him into giving her rich gifts instead.

Vladimir agreed. He ordered his subjects to be baptized, and told his boyars to give up worshiping Odin and Thor, and to burn their idols or cast them into the Dnepr River.

This conversion of the Slavs was as important to the Byzantines as a victory by their army or by their diplomats, and indeed it was a victory. For although they still fought with the Serbs and with the Russians and particularly with the Bulgarians, these people were gradually drawn into the Byzantine way of life and became more and more friendly. Thus the flanks of the empire were protected.

It was, of course, far more lasting than any military victory. The Byzantine Empire came to an end more than 500 years ago, but if you were to go into the Balkans or Greece today, you would find that the work done by Saint Cyril and Saint Methodius still remains. Even after forty years of communism, you might find that the seeds of Christianity, and particularly Greek Orthodox Christianity, which had been sown by Vladimir's conversion, were still living in some Russian communist hearts.

GOLDEN BEZANTS

It took a lot of money to be able to do all these things—to pay the expenses of the emperor and his court and government, and of the army, the navy, and the church, to say nothing of bribing foreign rulers and their ambassadors. And this money did not come from conquering fabulously rich lands and then making them hand over their treasures as tribute or as booty.

This method was the way the old Roman Empire had become wealthy. In fact, the famous Roman statesman Cicero, who had a rich province to govern, boasted to his friend Atticus that the natives loved him because he did not make them give him a well-furnished palace in every city where he spent the night. They thronged from every village and hamlet to cheer him because he did not force them to borrow money and then pay him back with forty-eight per cent interest!

81

But in Byzantine days there were very few fabulously rich countries left to conquer, and the Byzantines had to find some other source of wealth. They had to rely on hard work and on their own skill and cleverness. They supported themselves on the little farms that nestled in every Balkan valley and the huge estates that sprawled over Thrace and Anatolia (the Asiatic part of modern Turkey). They earned a living, sometimes even amassing treasure, in the many industries that were found in every Byzantine city. They became wealthy from their world-wide foreign trade.

Nobody can say today just how wealthy they were. One historian says that the Byzantine state had an annual budget of one hundred and twenty million dollars in gold, but another says that it was only twenty million.

No matter which was right, and it was probably the first, you would still have to multiply the figure many times to find out what it is worth in modern money. Anyway, this was only the money spent by the government; it did not include the vast sums and the enormous property owned by private citizens. There may have been fifteen million people in the Byzantine Empire, and while some of them were poor as poor could be, a great many of them were very rich indeed.

Of all ways of making a living, farming probably came first. Rich or poor, almost every Byzantine had an eye for the land, that is, everyone except the city mobs who couldn't bear to be too far away from the excitement of the Circus.

In fact, many people say that the reason the Byzantine Empire finally lost its wealth was because the average Byzantine preferred to invest his money in an estate rather than in foreign trade. The Byzantines let foreign trade fall into the hands of the Venetians, Genoese, and Pisans. Then when the Turks came and the richest provinces fell into the hands of the invaders, there was nothing to fall back on, and no money to pay soldiers to hold the Turks off.

If that is so, it was for the same reason that the Byzantines did not like the navy; foreign trade was too uncertain and there was no way to figure out your risks. Just take pirates alone. The Aegean Sea and in fact the whole eastern Mediterranean was strewn with islands behind which lurked swift ships, manned by swarthy corsairs. They were as dangerous as Captain Kidd or Henry Morgan, and they kept Byzantine traders terrified.

"What am I going to do?" jeered one of them, a Genoese, as he boarded a heavily laden Byzantine merchant vessel. "Seize you and your goods, *and cut off your noses!*"

But besides pirates, there was wind and weather, land robbers (if you shipped your goods by caravan), and the possibility that some prince or emir would confiscate your property and say that it was indemnity owed to him by the Byzantine Government.

And there was only the most primitive kind of insurance to take care of you in time of trouble.

Of course, farming had its difficulties and dangers too. The farmer was just as likely to have his crops ruined by drought or by heavy rains as he is today. Also just as today, prices were only high when there was little to sell. When the yield was plentiful and the farmer's storerooms were full, prices went down and so even if you sold a lot, you didn't get much in return. There were also wild beasts to contend with. The Balkans and Asia Minor were far more covered with waste and woodland than they are now, and you did not have to go to the steppes of Russia to find ravening wolf packs. No Byzantine herdsman dared go out without a sheepdog as savage as a wolf itself. Sheepdogs were so important that a man who killed one was given 100 lashes and had to pay double the dog's value to its owner. Life was often hard for the Byzantine farmer. We must never think of the world in those days being like it is today. Boundary lines were not rigidly fixed with customs officials at every point, and even when the Byzantine Empire was strongest, savage bands and even nations crossed the Danube and other rivers, roving to their hearts' content. They never captured Constantinople, and the big cities of the empire—from Thessalonica and Athens to Antioch and Berytus (modern Beirut)—were often safe. But a farmer who came back from his fields was just as likely to find his farmhouse a smoking ruin and his wife and children murdered or carried off, as a settler in our own wilderness days was to find them scalped by Indians. The conditions were about the same.

Nevertheless, at least in most periods, and in a great many parts of the empire, the Byzantine farmer did prosper and was not only able to feed the empire but to ship some of his surplus abroad as well.

This Byzantine farmer was very versatile. He grew wheat, olives, every kind of fruit, and even flax and cotton. He maintained herds of goats and sheep and cattle and horses. In his "more or less self-governing" villages, there was not only uncleared woodland, scrubby wastes, and unfenced pastures, but vineyards and garden patches protected by deep ditches and palisades of pointed stakes.

The very existence of a special farmer's law shows how important he was. This law took care of everything from stealing or killing livestock to accidentally plowing someone else's land. The man who did this lost his crop and also the time he had spent.

Another thing that shows how important the farmer was

to the Byzantine Empire is 'the size of a medium-sized farm: 100 yoke of oxen, 500 grazing oxen, 80 horses or mules, 12,000 sheep. That was what could be found on a typical farm!

Indeed, the main difficulties faced by the Byzantine farmer were taxes, and the greediness of the big landowners. Taxes were high and if one man did not pay them, the whole village was responsible for his share. The greedy big landowner caused even more trouble. Some of these "robbers in silk and velvet," as they were called, owned estates as big as provinces, but even that did not satisfy them and they spent much of their time trying to get the land of the neighboring small farmers.

They tried all sorts of tricks and schemes. For instance, if a small farmer was sick or in trouble, his rich neighbor would offer to help him out if the farmer would adopt him as his son. Then when the small farmer died, the rich farmer inherited the land, and the small farmer's wife and his real children could beg or become farm hands or slaves. Finally, an emperor who had been a small farmer himself made a law to protect the small farmer. From then on the small farmer was not allowed to give, sell, or even lease his land to a big farmer. But this law did not last for long. The big farmer had too much influence and had it repealed.

Next to farming in importance was Byzantine industry, and in the long run this probably produced more wealth than the Byzantine farmers did.

It was, of course, necessary to feed the huge city population, and in spite of all the produce grown and raised on their farms, the Byzantines still had to import some of the things they needed. Wheat was one of them, and sometimes salt fish, wine, and of course slaves.

It was also necessary to clothe the people, make shoes for

them, butcher their meat, bake their bread, cask wine for them, and build and furnish their houses. This kept many hands busy.

But it was the luxury trades that brought the Byzantines their fame and fortune. The goldsmiths made gold cups and chalices, gold inlaid silver patens and plates, gold pectoral crosses (the cross worn by a churchman upon his breast). They also made jewelry and enamel that was so beautiful that people still say that the finest and most exquisite craftsmanship of the Middle Ages was Byzantine.

The glassmakers made their famous Byzantine glass. It was noted for its rich color, and no other glass equaled it until the Venetians began making glass on the neighboring island of Murano in 1291. There was a special kind of Byzantine glass called *fonde d'oro*. In this, designs of pure gold were put between two layers of glass and then fused together.

The Byzantines also made and exported the finest kind of china, ivory carved with figures of saints and emperors, vases of honey-colored agate, lawn and other delicate cloth, perfumes, strange and sharp-smelling mixtures of spices and herbs, and too many other things to mention. These Byzantine goods went all over the world. Byzantine products have been found even in Scotland.

But perhaps the most important of all Byzantine industries was the silk industry. Byzantine silks and heavy gold brocade were not only needed throughout the empire for church services and imperial functions. They, too, were widely shipped abroad.

In the days of the old Roman Empire, all silk came from China, where Roman ambassadors had traveled 1,000 years before Marco Polo. The silk was carried by caravan across the desert to Samarkand, and then to the Persian border, where heavy duty had to be paid on it.

Silk still came from China—and there was still a heavy duty on it—in the early days of the Byzantine Empire. But one day while Justinian sat on his throne two Christian monks appeared before him, one of them holding in his hand a hollow bamboo. He broke it open, and inside were silkworm cocoons. They had been smuggled all the way from distant Canton or Nanking.

From then on, the Byzantines had a silk industry of their own. The silkworm was cultivated all over the empire, but especially in the Peloponnesus, the peninsula of southern Greece, which now became known as the Morea—the Latin word for mulberry leaf is *morus*—from the mulberry trees grown there for the silkworms to feed upon. Silk cloth was woven all over the empire, but principally in Greece and at Constantinople.

As a matter of fact, some silk was even manufactured upon the very grounds of the imperial Sacred Palace. This was a special royal silk, and it was illegal to take any of it from the empire.

Bishop Liutprand of Cremona—the same one who saw the emperor magically lifted up into the air at the Magnaura Palace—tried to smuggle some out of Constantinople, but he was caught.

He tried to bluff his way through the customs by roaring, "Your emperor Nicephorus came to his throne by lying and crime! He told me I could buy all that I wanted to. Where is the imperial promise?"

But although Liutprand was an ambassador from the German emperor, the Byzantines merely smiled at him.

"You poverty-stricken Italians and Germans are not meant to appear in such gorgeous material. Only we Byzantines, who are unique in virtue, have a right to wear them."

They forced him to open his baggage and took five of the most splendid pieces. But they did pay him back the money he had spent.

None of this Byzantine silk, and none of the other marvelous things they made either, would have added very much to Byzantine gold and glitter if the Byzantines had kept all for themselves. Little as the average Byzantine liked to risk his money in foreign adventures, it was foreign trade that brought most of their wealth.

Byzantine foreign trade reached out all over the world. The Byzantines imported animal skins, slaves, and sometimes wheat from Russia; precious stones from India; spices from Ceylon; embroidered rugs from Spain and Morocco; ores and wrought metals from Italy and Germany; wool and woolen goods from the Low Countries and England; hemp, flax, and amber from the Balkans and the north. These were only a few things they imported. Some of these things were shipped out again; for instance, they shipped amber from the Baltic to the Far East.

The Byzantines even penetrated darkest Africa. Not only did they do business with the Ethiopian kingdom of Axum on the Red Sea where the temperature sometimes went up to 120°, but they may even have gone with the dark-skinned Axumite merchants to the mysterious city of Zambabwe. There, in the heart of the jungle, Negro tribesmen built towers, walls, and palaces so mighty that even today men look at the ruins and wonder how they did it.

Gold seemed to be as plentiful as pebbles in Zambabwe, and you traded with the natives in the following way: You built a thick thorn breastwork, and on it you placed salt, iron, and the carcasses of cattle. Then you went away, and the natives slipped out of the forest and placed beans of gold upon each object. Later on you came back and if you thought they had left enough, you took the gold and the natives carried off the meat and salt and iron. If not, you moved away and the natives were given a chance to leave more gold. Sometimes this bartering went on for four or five days. Neither side saw, or even talked to, the other.

The Byzantines were able to carry on this world business, because their principal city, Constantinople, had one of the most strategic locations in the known world of that time. It was like a spider in the center of a spider web; practically every trade route in the world passed through it.

The Byzantines also had a large number of unusually fine seaports in other parts of the empire. Besides Constantinople itself, there was Smyrna, Thessalonica, Patras, and in the early days, Alexandria. There were several others, many of which are very good seaports even today.

The Byzantines also knew how to promote business. We are apt to think of a world's fair as something modern, but the Byzantines knew all about them. Every year, in October, they held an enormous trade fair on the Vardar plain outside Thessalonica. There they built a huge temporary wood-and-canvas city of booths and bazaars, and even amid the troubled Middle Ages, merchants and peddlers flocked to it from all over. It was only later, when the Byzantines became proud and haughty, refusing to seek business while they sat on their doorsteps waiting for business to come to them, that they got into trouble. Then the energetic Venetians, Genoese, and Pisans took over.

But nothing had more to do with making the Byzantines

GOLD  BEZANT

successful in world trade than the sound Byzantine money. Their gold coin, known to us as the bezant, was one of the four most widely accepted pieces of money the world has ever known. The other three are the Florentine florin, which made the Medici bankers so rich, the English pound sterling, and now the United States dollar. Any one of these would be accepted anywhere in the world during the time it was in use.

The reason the Byzantine coin was stable is that no one ever tampered with the bezant. In the old days, kings used

to clip their coins (that is, use a little less gold in them), but no emperor ever clipped the bezant. It was always kept at its full value.

An old Byzantine writer tells a story which shows both how valuable the bezant was and how it traveled.

A Greek merchant was in Ceylon when he got into an argument with a Persian merchant as to whose ruler was the more powerful.

"Mine," said the Persian. "He is King of Kings."

"Why argue?" asked the Greek. "They are both in the room. Compare them."

"What do you mean?"

"Well, I have some bezants, and you have some dirhams. Put them beside each other."

There was no need for further discussion. The portrait of the *basileus* of the Romans was on the bezant, and the bezant was the much more valuable coin.

I, myself, had an experience which proves the same thing. On my desk in front of me is a real Byzantine gold piece. It was coined in the reign of Basil I and his son Constantine, and cannot be a day less than 1,090 years old. But I was able to buy it at a price that I could afford. I asked the coin dealer why.

"Bezants were used all over the world, and so you find them everywhere!" he answered.

Because the Byzantine emperors made their gold coins so stable in value that everybody wanted them, I am able to own one today!

THE BYZANTINE
WAY OF LIFE

What did the Byzantine Empire do for itself, and for the world, and even for us, during the eleven long centuries when it was almost always—but not *always*—so rich and powerful?

You would not really know about the Byzantines unless you had the answer.

First of all, it defended a large part of the warm, civilized Mediterranean lands from the Asiatic barbarians. The word "Asiatic" is important, but maybe "barbarians from the Asiatic steppes" would be better, for these were barbarians of a special kind.

Our ancestors were barbarians, too, and the barbarians that came from the forests of Germany and the sandy shores of Denmark were capable of cruel destruction. But they were also free and independent, with a gift for self-government and an instinct that told them that one man has just as many rights as another. They even elected their kings, cheering and lifting them on their shields, and the kings they elected were men like Theodoric of Italy, Alfred the Great, and Charlemagne, all men who wanted to absorb the very best of the civilization they had taken over, and not merely tear things down.

If, instead of them, men like Attila and Genghis Khan, with their hard-riding, slant-eyed followers, had become the rulers of western Europe, iron discipline and a firm government might have been established a whole lot sooner. But our democratic way of living could never have been born. In other words, the Byzantines defended Europe from the Asiatic hordes and made it possible for Western civilization to develop in its own way.

The Byzantines would hardly be worth remembering if they had done nothing more than defend.

They also created a civilization of their own, and you can still see its influence in Yugoslavia, Bulgaria, Greece, Romania, and even Russia. And there are still traces of it all over Europe and Asia.

If a Byzantine had come to life and looked at the coronation of Elizabeth II of England over TV, he would have felt perfectly at home, for in many ways it was a Byzantine ceremony. The fact that this young woman was not only sovereign of the realm but head of the official church was Byzantine, too. She was following in the footsteps of the empresses Irene and Zoe.

In the East, even the Turks who finally conquered the Byzantines took over many of their ideas. In its early days the Turkish Empire was very much like the Byzantine Empire, except that it practiced Islam, the religion founded by Mohammed. The Turkish *sanjaks,* or provinces, had almost the same boundaries as the Byzantine *themes,* or provinces. Their grand vizier, or prime minister—but there is a difference, for the vizier's name means "he who bears burdens," rather than "accountant"—was practically the same as the Logothete of the Dromos. A Turkish *bey* was not too different from a Byzantine *strategos,* or governor general.

The Turks even used Byzantines to help them rule. A large number of the governors whom they sent out to their conquered territories were Phanariote Greeks, those Greeks who remained in Constantinople after the empire fell. All but twelve of their forty-eight grand viziers were either Byzantines or from former Byzantine provinces such as Albania, Dalmatia, or Greece.

Byzantine civilization affected much more of daily life than merely ceremonies and government, however. It entered into every phase of life. It was the Byzantines who invented the fork. From Constantinople it was taken to Italy, and medieval English tourists brought it back to Britain. But for a long time a man was considered sissy and affected if he used one instead of his fingers.

High on the list of the great accomplishments of the Byzantines is Byzantine art. In fact, many people think of it first, and sometimes it is the only thing they think about when they think of the Byzantines. Not long ago it was not very much appreciated, but we now realize that it is one of the finest arts there ever was. Besides that, it bridged the more than thousand-year gap in art between the wonderful statues of the Greeks and Romans and the oil paintings and frescoes of the Italian Renaissance.

The most famous Byzantine art is the Byzantine mosaics. A Byzantine mosaic is a picture made of little pieces of glass and gold and precious stones. These mosaics were usually

very large and set right into the walls of churches, and so it is almost impossible to see one unless you visit the church itself. You would have to go at least to Italy where there are some very fine ones in Rome, Ravenna, and Naples. These Byzantine mosaics are quite stiff, and the people in them usually look straight ahead. But if you ever see a real one, or even a good picture of one, you will never forget it.

The Byzantines also did oil paintings and frescoes, particularly in their later days and particularly in the Balkans and Greece. There are frescoes in Yugoslavia and in southern Greece that are almost as good as those of the great Italian artist Giotto, and they were done 200 years before him. Byzantine sculpture ranged from richly carved marble, like the big throne of a patriarch in Ravenna, to ivory caskets and plaques. Byzantine illuminated manuscripts are also among the most beautiful ever made. Most of them are Bibles and other religious books, but there are several about the travels of Cosmas Who-Sailed-to-India. They are filled with saints in blue and scarlet, and one manuscript has a picture of a boatload of escaping martyrs showing what travel was like in Byzantine days.

Byzantine art is not only wonderful itself, but it shows how the Byzantines helped themselves to everything good that had been done before them. On the walls of a famous tomb in Ravenna, there is a mosaic of two doves at a drinking fountain that might have come from the ancient Roman city of Pompeii. There is also Byzantine art that bubbles over with Greek love of life. Some of it is filled with early Christian saints and symbols, like the peacock and the fish. There is some with the lions and eagles of the ancient Hittites, and others whose fierce, bearded saints are like Assyrian warriors. But, of course, this practice of blending the ideas of different peoples wasn't limited to art. It applied to everything the Byzantines did.

The Byzantines preserved classic culture. They preserved Greek literature, Greek science, Greek learning, and even the Greek language. And this at a time when almost everybody in the West had completely forgotten Greek, and as a matter of fact, only churchmen and a handful of ragged scholars even knew Latin.

This was a very important contribution. No civilization ever starts from scratch, and our modern one is based on the renewed interest in classic culture that is called the Revival of Learning. During that time, great writers like Petrarch and Boccaccio were willing to spend a fortune to get the services of some bearded ruffian who could teach them Greek. When Constantinople fell, the Byzantine scholars who escaped to Europe could sell any manuscript they brought with them for enough money to live on for a long time.

The Byzantines never had to rediscover Homer, or Plato, or Euclid, who invented geometry, or Eratosthenes, who knew the world was round 1,700 years before Columbus, even measuring its circumference as 25,000 miles, which is almost right. They never had to rediscover the ancients; they knew about them all the time.

Another thing the Byzantines did was to insist on education. Even the mighty French emperor Charlemagne had a hard time if he wanted to spell his way through a book and sign his name. Most Byzantine emperors could not only read and write but were thoroughly educated. Theophilus studied everything from Greek to natural history. Leo the Philosopher composed poems, sermons, and a life of his father. Constantine Born-in-the-Purple was famous for his books on the barbarians and on his empire. John IV and Manuel II, and above all Anna Comnena, a princess, wrote astonishingly good histories.

It was not merely the emperors and some of their courtiers who were learned. Although a few poor men—like the saint from Asia Minor who had to tend his father's swine and did not learn to read until he was forty-seven—did not have the chance to be educated, most Byzantines went to school or a university from the time they were five until they were twenty.

If you had been a Byzantine, you would have trotted off to your classes accompanied by a pedagogue—in the old days, he was a slave—who carried your books and saw to it that you obeyed your teachers. Until you were ten, you would have studied reading, writing, and spelling. The last was very important because the way words were pronounced was always changing, although the spelling remained the same. After this you would have studied what the Byzantines called grammar. But it was not exactly like our grammar. It was more like literature. For instance, you would have had to learn Homer by heart and been able to explain everything he had written word by word. You were in trouble if you weren't able to do this. The teacher merely nodded to the pedagogue, who always had a rod in his hand. After grammar, you would have studied rhetoric, and to pass your rhetoric courses you had to be able to discuss eloquently anything from a fable by Aesop to the pictures on the walls of the city council. Finally, and this was especially important if you were going to be a churchman or go into the government, you would have gone on to a university. That was the case only if you were a boy. Although many Byzantine women were as well educated as the men, everything they learned was in the home. None of them went to college or even to grammar school.

Besides giving us great art, keeping alive Greek culture and civilization, and seeing to it that there was at least one place in the world where everyone who wanted to be was educated, the Byzantines protected and preserved the Christian faith.

Long before the word "crusader" was ever heard, the Byzantine emperor Heraclius was fighting the Saracens in Damascus, Homs, Jerusalem, and Antioch just as the crusaders did in the days of Richard the Lion-Hearted 500 years later. Almost every Byzantine emperor who followed him did the same. Among the caliphs whom they fought, but could not defeat, was Harun al-Rashid, the hero of *The Arabian Nights*.

They did defeat many another Moslem leader, however, and so although the Arabs often advanced through the empire, they were never able to pour into the Balkans as they had poured into France and Spain.

But the Byzantines did more than just battle the enemies of Christianity, and they also did more than argue over the fine points of religion.

They tried to practice Christianity as well as preach it. They believed that *philanthropia*—from which our word "philanthropy," or "love of mankind" is derived—was the first duty of those who were rich or had power. There were no people before the Byzantines, and only a few since, who believed so sincerely that every man was really and truly his brother's keeper. And by being his brother's keeper they meant taking care of him in every kind of need.

In the Byzantine Empire there were homes for travelers and pilgrims. There were homes for orphans. There were homes for the sick. There were homes for foundlings. There were old-age homes.

All of these institutions were heavily endowed when they

were not actually supported by the government, and the officials in charge of them were important people. Take the orphan homes, for example. There were forty orphan homes in Constantinople alone. Each was headed by an *orphanotrope*. The Grand Orphanotrope who was over all of them, was appointed by the emperor himself. He held one of the highest offices in the empire.

Many of the Byzantine laws were Christian as well. In the old days of the ancient Roman Empire, the father was the absolute master of the family. His wife's property, including her dowry, became his, and if he did not like her, he could divorce her with little more than a word. At least in the very early days, he had power of life and death over his slaves and almost as much over his children. If a son did not please him, he did not have to leave him a penny in his will.

But the Byzantines did not want laws like that. They wanted laws that the Saviour would approve of. In their opinion, Christ would not have approved of divorce, and so although they could not stop it altogether, they made it much more difficult to get. At one time there were only four recognized reasons for divorce. One of them was that you could get a divorce if your husband (or wife) tried to murder you!

Women were given many other rights by the Byzantines. If a child wanted to marry, he had to get his mother's permission as well as his father's. A woman's property did not belong exclusively to her husband; her property and her husband's property now belonged to both of them. If the father died, the mother could become her child's guardian.

The child also got some new advantages. If you got a job in the old Roman days, your earnings went to your father. Under the Byzantines, you could keep them yourself.

Slaves also had to be treated with justice. Under Christianity, even the most wretched slave was a human being with a soul which he could lose or save. He was no longer cattle, and his master could not slay him at will. He could not even treat him inhumanely.

Even the laws about business were based on the idea that the good of everybody was more important than the good of any individual. In fact, the Byzantines had an almost socialistic control of everything and everybody that made money.

Every branch of Byzantine industry was organized into corporations or guilds, and these corporations had the right to fix prices and wages down to the last penny. They had the right to decide who could go into a trade or business. They had the right to decide the exact place where a shop or booth or factory could be set up; for example, no shop selling wax and candles could be less than seventy yards from another candle shop. They also had the right to decide what goods could be imported, and what kind of goods, and in what amounts, could be shipped abroad.

But even at that, the corporations did not have absolute control of everything, for over them was the *eparch,* or lord mayor, and over the *eparch* was the emperor.

The emperor was supposed to be for all of the people and not for any group of them, and the emperor had the last word.

In spite of all they accomplished and their charitable principles and humane ideas, the Byzantines also had faults, however. There was a black side to their civilization just as there was a bright side, and some of it was very black indeed.

The Byzantines were very cruel. They were Greek, but they were also Oriental, and had in them a ferocious streak that not only was indifferent to suffering but seemed to take a fiendish pleasure in it. Most mobs are savage, but the Byzantine mob was even more savage than usual. Only the mobs of the French Revolution can compare with it.

For instance, when the Byzantines overthrew the emperor Andronicus, they were not satisfied with just tossing him from his throne. A howling crowd of men and women tore out his beard, broke his teeth, beat him, and dragged him through the streets at the tail of a mangy camel while shouting fearful curses at him. He was seventy years old, but although he begged to be put out of his misery, it was many hours before a soldier who was not one of the crowd took pity on him and killed him.

He was by no means the only emperor who died cruelly. As a matter of fact, it was a very rare thing for an emperor to die peacefully in his bed. Usurpers and would-be emperors were often treated just as savagely as Andronicus had been.

Byzantine laws could be cruel, too, although their cruelty was in the name of Christianity and mercy. The Byzantines thought it was against the teachings of Christ to condemn a man to death, and so the death penalty was rare. Instead, a criminal was mutilated; they tore out his tongue or cut off his nose or a hand. Blinding was a common punishment. The Byzantines actually thought it was merciful to blind a man instead of executing him.

The Byzantines were treacherous, and, in fact, "Byzantine treachery" became a well-known saying. Probably they were not as treacherous as their enemies said they were, and their enemies, including the crusaders, were also treacherous. But in everyday life just as when they went to war, the Byzantines were always ready to plot, trick, deceive, and lie. When they did tell the truth, it was usually because honesty happened to be the best policy, and not because they thought that honesty was the only right thing.

The emperors often gained the throne by trickery. Michael the Drunkard made Basil I his co-emperor in the kingdom because Basil had deceived him into thinking that Michael's uncle, the *Caesar* Bardas, was a traitor. *Caesar* Bardas was executed. Then Basil waited until Michael was asleep, and had him murdered.

Michael's grandfather, Michael the Stutterer, had come to the throne in the same way. As a matter of fact, he was in prison when he succeeded in outwitting a boyhood companion who was then the emperor. He actually still had chains on his wrists and ankles when he was crowned.

The Byzantines were corrupt and prospered on graft. Although most of this graft and corruption centered around the imperial court, business and the church were often corrupt. In all three of these places, you got ahead by giving—and receiving—favors.

The Byzantines were high-strung, excitable, and fiery.

The Byzantines were very fond of luxury whether in dress, food, jewelry, furniture, or even horses and chariots.

They craved entertainment. One emperor even told his signalmen not to light the beacons that carried news of an approaching enemy from hill to hill until it reached Constantinople. He was afraid it would cast gloom upon the horse races.

The Byzantines were much too fond of pleasure.

Even so, when you add the pluses and subtract the minuses for the Byzantines, it turns out that you have something pretty good, particularly for those troubled times.

Besides, not all the Byzantines were unprincipled and evil. The mob at the bottom and the courtiers and noblemen on top had glaring defects, but the middle-class Byzantines, of whom there were more than any other group, were often brave, high-spirited, and loyal; and they were always intelligent. The Byzantine father was steady and hard-working, and the mother sincerely pious and devoted to her children. Their life was sometimes hard, but it was often happy. And there always was a chance for self-respect.

LAST DAYS OF THE EMPIRE

Geoffrey of Villehardouin and Robert of Clari—the two writer-crusaders—were among the last people to see Constantinople in all its glory, and even they were not able to walk through streets filled with magnificence for very long.

The knights and barons of the Fourth Crusade had promised to put the young Alexius on the throne. This they did, and for good measure they put his old blinded father back on the throne beside him too. They let the rulers wear the imperial purple shoes and the glittering brocaded robes, pretending to have restored the imperial power. Alexius and his father could indeed wield the scepter and wear the crown and be absolute monarchs, provided they did everything the crusaders told them to.

In return, the young Alexius had promised to pay the crusaders 200,000 marks of silver, to lead an army to the Holy

Land with them, and to maintain and equip 500 of their knights in armor for as long as he lived.

This, however, was another matter, and when the two emperors made even a half-hearted attempt to live up to their promises, the Byzantines revolted. Another Alexius—Alexius Bushy Eyebrows—was made emperor and he made it known that the Venetians and the crusaders could whistle for their money. Not a single copper coin, let alone 200,000 silver ones, would they ever get from him!

This gave the crusaders the chance they had long been waiting for and probably planning for, and they didn't waste any time in taking it. Proclaiming Bushy Eyebrows, as they called him, a traitor and a caitiff villain, they attacked the city with ships, ladders, and men-at-arms. On April 13, 1204, after five days of desperate fighting, they burst into it. There for three days and nights, the Christian soldiers—wearing the

cross upon their shoulders—burned, robbed, and murdered the Christian Byzantines.

"Even the followers of Mahound, the false prophet, were more merciful when they took Jerusalem!" cried a Byzantine.

He was right. Little like it has ever happened anywhere else, except during the invasions of Attila the Hun. Constantinople has never been the same since.

The robbery was even more wholesale than the slaying. Churches, private homes, and palaces were stripped to their bare stone walls, and then all that was not hidden by private looters was piled where it could be seen and divided.

"The booty was so great that no one could tell you of it," said Villehardouin.

It included gold and silver; vessels and precious stones; silk and samite; robes of vair and robes of ermine; rare and irreplaceable books; icons; beautiful carved chests; and, of course, all the coinage in the treasury. In fact, everything that was not too heavy to move.

The Venetians were immediately paid the 50,000 marks reckoned to be their share. Even after that, not counting what had been stolen and hidden, there may have been 400,000 silver marks' worth of rare prizes. To say nothing— and there was no knight who didn't want one—of 10,000 fiery steeds!

There was no one who was too lofty or too pious to take his share of this booty. The abbots and the warrior-bishops laid their hands on every holy relic they could find. Most of these went to France, where they disappeared during the French Revolution. The doge took the four famous bronze horses of the Hippodrome, and even today the Venetians point to them on the façade of the church of Saint Mark just as proudly as if they had not helped themselves to them.

There was hardly a knight who did not wear rich fur-trimmed robes. There was hardly a common foot soldier or even a jackallike camp follower who did not have a fat purse, and a heavy chain of gold to boot. The proud Byzantines returned to ruined churches and to charred and plundered houses. Fabled Byzantium had become an empty shell.

The Byzantine Empire became an empty shell too. The crusaders captured the new emperor and made him jump from the top of one of the tall marble columns. Then, after a lot of bickering, they elected one of their own number to succeed him. There was an empire, but it was now a Latin empire and no one but the crusaders recognized it. Even they did not leave it all its territory. Venice took over a third of Constantinople and most of the Byzantine islands in the Aegean and Ionian seas. Every knight or baron who wanted it was given a fief or a principality in southern Greece. Besides that, three Byzantine "governments in exile," each claiming to be the real one, sprang into being. One was at Trebizond near the eastern end of the Black Sea. One was in Epirus, which is more or less the same as modern Albania. The third and most important was at Nicaea, which was just across the straights in Asia Minor.

So for fifty-seven years, there was not one Byzantine Empire, but four of them, plus half a dozen other small states that all squabbled with each other. Then, in 1261, Michael Paleologus, a great-grandson of one of the old emperors recaptured Constantinople and put on the imperial crown.

But although there was only one Byzantine Empire again, it was little more than a shadow. Nor could any of the nine Byzantine emperors who followed Michael restore the old-time glory. The crusaders had done too good a job. Constantinople was now too poor and shabby. Its trade was gone. Its famous bazaars were filthy, and their booths were empty of wares. Most of the population had moved away. Even the emperors themselves lived hand to mouth. Although they tried to keep up the ancient ceremony, they couldn't do it. At the wedding of a daughter of one of the emperors, the guests had to eat off earthenware plates.

Besides that, and probably because of it, anarchy reigned during the 200 years that the empire somehow lingered drearily on. Mercenary bands moved about the countryside robbing and stealing, instead of fighting for the emperor. They even moved on Constantinople when they weren't paid, or thought they were not paid enough.

The Byzantines also had to fight off outside enemies. The Bulgarians renewed their old-time warfare and nibbled away at the shrinking empire. A great Serbian king proclaimed himself Roman emperor as well as Serbian monarch. He almost succeeded. The Byzantines had to fight the Genoese, and sometimes the Venetians, and even the Frank barons, descendants of the crusaders.

Finally the Ottoman Turks appeared upon the scene, and that was the last blow. These wonderful fighters conquered all of Anatolia and then step by step they worked their way into Europe. It was not long before the Byzantine Empire was only Constantinople itself with a few square miles of the surrounding countryside. The Byzantines soon couldn't even raise an army without Turkish permission, and usually that permission wasn't granted.

In 1453, which is one of the famous dates in history, even that much freedom seemed too much to the Turks, and their young ambitious sultan, Mohammed II, decided to take the city. Slowly and carefully he laid plans to do so.

First he built one tower here and another there, ringing

the city and cutting off escape from it. Then he brought up a mighty navy of 493 ships, and a great army of 200,000 men. It was the first army in history to be equipped with siege guns, and one of these was so big it took 100 oxen to drag it. Mohammed, too, was so determined to take Constantinople that when his ships could not break through the iron chain the Byzantines had laid across the Golden Horn, he had a whole fleet of them dragged overland, with the crew still sitting at the oars—and all this in a single night.

What could the Byzantines do against all this power? They had only 8,000 soldiers, and many of these were monks and untrained citizens. To be sure, they were led by two heroes, one an Italian mercenary, the other the last Byzantine emperor, Constantine XI. Both of them heroically lost their lives in the battle to defend Constantinople.

But heroism was not enough, and the city's walls, mighty as they were, could be smashed by cannon balls. After a month of siege the howling Janizaries entered it. Once again, Constantinople was sacked and looted, and although the Turks were not nearly so ruthless as the crusaders had been, this time it did not rise again.

The empire did not rise again either. On May 29, 1453, Constantinople, which had once been Byzantium, became Istanbul. It has been Istanbul ever since.

On that day, the Byzantine Empire ended too.

For more than a thousand years, it had carried the torch of Western civilization, a torch that had been given to it by the Greeks and Romans. Now, new nations took up the burden. Spain, France, and England had become united and powerful. Italy was filled with all the wonderful art and thought and writing and wealth that came with the Italian Renaissance. Germany was stirring with new ideas. Even in distant

Poland, Copernicus would soon be looking through his telescope and teaching us that the sun did not revolve around the earth, but rather that the planets revolve around the sun. In only forty years Columbus would discover America.

So their job became our job, and it still is. They were not perfect, but let us hope that we do it as well as they did. Let us hope that our civilization lasts as long.

CHRONOLOGICAL CHART
OF
THE BYZANTINE EMPIRE
AND
WORLD EVENTS

	BYZANTINE WORLD	ENGLAND AND WESTERN EUROPE
A.D. 300–400	Constantine the Great establishes capital of Roman Empire at Constantinople on site of ancient Byzantium, 330	Teutonic and Asiatic barbarians overrun Roman Empire
	First division of Roman Empire into East and West, 364	
	Final division of Roman Empire into East and West, 395	
400–500		Visigoths sack Rome, 410
		Huns under Attila invade Europe, 445–453
	Period of decline	Western Europe lost to Roman Empire
		First Saxon kingdom in Britain, 477: Clovis I founds Frank kingdom in France, 481
500–600	Justinian the Great (Great advancement of Byzantine civilization), 527–565	Beginning of modern Western European civilization
	Laws codified	
	Empire reaches greatest territorial extent (from Spain to Persia)	
	Santa Sophia built, 532–537	
	First great age of Byzantine art	
600–700	Persians defeated by Heraclius, 641; end of Persian dominion	
	Byzantines drive Arabs away from Constantinople with "Greek fire," 677	
700–800	Iconoclast controversy; image worship forbidden by Leo the Isaurian, 726	Charles Martel defeats Moslems at Tours, France, 732; stops Arab expansion into Europe
800–900	Image worship restored, 843	Charlemagne crowned emperor of Holy Roman Empire at Rome, 800
	Byzantine missionaries convert Bulgarians to Orthodox Christianity, 864	
	Macedonian dynasty (founded by Basil I), 867–1056	
	Second great advancement of Byzantine civilization	

	NEAR EAST AND ASIA	WESTERN HEMISPHERE
A.D. 300–400	Successive wars between Persians and Romans Golden Age of Hinduism in India Divided empire in China (Tartar and Chinese rule)	
400–500		
500–600		
600–700	Beginning of Arab Empire, 632 Byzantines defeat Persians, 641; end of Persian dominion	
700–800	Moslem defeat at Tours, 732, stops Arab expansion into Europe Golden Age of Arab Empire, 750–1258: Revival of Chinese Empire under T'ang dynasty	
800–900	Bulgarians converted to Orthodox Christianity, 864 Beginning of Russia	

	BYZANTINE WORLD	ENGLAND AND WESTERN EUROPE
A.D. 900–1000		Arab rule in Spain at height; Cordova greatest intellectual center in Europe
	Russians converted to Orthodox Christianity, 989	
1000–1100	Basil II conquers Bulgarians; rules from Asia Minor to southern Italy, 1014	William the Conqueror invades England, 1066
	Defeat by Seljuk Turks in Armenia, 1071; decline of Byzantine military power	Crusades against Moslems in Holy Lands, 1096–1270
1100–1200	Comnenus dynasty unable to restore Byzantine power	
1200–1300	Crusaders take Constantinople, 1204	Magna Charta in England, 1215
	Michael VIII reconquers Constantinople; restores Greek rule, 1261	
1300–1400	Ottoman Turks invade Europe, defeat Serbs, 1389; Byzantine Empire reduced to Constantinople and surroundings	
1400–1500	Tamerlane defeats Ottoman Turks at Ankara, 1402; delays fall of Byzantine Empire	Renaissance
	John VIII agrees to unite Greek and Roman churches to gain Western aid, 1439; plan fails	Invention of printing, 1439
	Ottoman Turks capture Constantinople; end of Byzantine Empire, 1453	

A.D.	NEAR EAST AND ASIA	WESTERN HEMISPHERE
900–1000	Arab rule in Spain at height; Cordova greatest intellectual center in Europe	Maya civilization in Mexico and Central America
	Russians converted to Orthodox Christianity, 989	Eric the Red discovers Greenland, about 985
1000–1100	Baghdad seized by Seljuk Turks, 1055	Leif Ericson visits America (Vinland), about 1000
	Crusades against Moslems in Holy Lands, 1096–1270	
	Jerusalem captured by crusaders, 1099	
1100–1200		
1200–1300	Genghis Khan conquers central Asia and China, 1206–1221	Inca civilization in Peru
	Mongols destroy Baghdad; overthrow Arab Empire, 1258	
	Marco Polo at court of Kublai Khan in China, 1271–1295	
	Ottoman Empire (Turks) founded, 1288	
1300–1400	Tamerlane ruler of Asia from Russia to Persian Gulf, 1369–1405	Aztec civilization in Mexico
1400–1500		
	Ottoman Turks conquer most of Asia; block trade routes to Far East	
	Moors expelled from Spain: Beginning of Spanish exploration in New World	Columbus discovers America, 1492

BOOKS FOR FURTHER READING

Baynes, Norman H., *The Byzantine Empire*. New York, Oxford University Press, Inc., 1926.

Diehl, Charles, *Byzantium: Greatness and Decline*. New Brunswick, Rutgers University Press, 1957.

Duggan, Alfred, *The Lady for Ransom*. New York, Coward-McCann, Inc., 1954.

Hussey, J. M., *The Byzantine World*. New York, Rinehart & Company, Inc., 1957.

Kielty, Bernardine, *The Fall of Constantinople*. New York, Random House, 1957.

Lamb, Harold, *Constantinople: The Birth of an Empire*. New York, Alfred A. Knopf, Inc., 1957.

———, *Theodora and the Emperor: The Drama of Justinian*. Garden City, Doubleday & Company, Inc., 1952.

Masefield, John, *Conquer, A Tale of the Nika Rebellion in Byzantium*. New York, The Macmillan Co., 1941.

Schoonover, Lawrence, *The Gentle Infidel*. New York, The Macmillan Co., 1950.

Scott, Walter, *Count Robert*. New York, The Macmillan Co., 1953.

INDEX AND GLOSSARY

ABOUT THE AUTHOR

THOMAS CALDECOT CHUBB, internationally known author, scholar, and literary critic began his writing career while still a student at Yale with the publication of two books, one of which won him the Albert Stanborough Cook award for poetry, and a poem which won him the John Masefield Award. Since that time he has published a number of books which are outstanding for both scholarship and writing—among these his well-known biography *Aretino: Scourge of Princes*. Mr. Chubb's interest in the Byzantines, awakened during his college days, has continued throughout his life. *The Byzantines*, his first book for young people, reflects his intimate knowledge of the subject.

World traveler, sportsman, and civic leader, Mr. Chubb lives in Greenwich, Connecticut, with his wife and their three teen-age children.